PREACHING THROUGH
THE LIFE OF CHRIST

Hendrickson Preaching Series

PREACHING THROUGH THE LIFE OF CHRIST

D. W. CLEVERLEY FORD

HENDRICKSON
PUBLISHERS
PEABODY, MASSACHUSETTS 01961-3473

First published 1985 by Mowbray, a Cassell imprint, London

PREACHING THROUGH THE LIFE OF CHRIST

© A. R. Mowbray & Co. Ltd 1985

Hendrickson Publishers, Inc., Edition 1994

ISBN 1-56563-044-0

Reprinted by arrangement with Mowbray,
an imprint of Cassell plc, London.

Printed in the United States of America

To the memory
of
TERESA CHILD
friend and fellow-worker

Expecto resurrectionem

ACKNOWLEDGEMENTS

I wish to record my thanks to Messrs A. R. Mowbray & Co. Ltd, the publishers, for the invitation to write this book; to the Reverend Michael Bourdeaux, of Keston College for permission to quote from his book *Risen Indeed*, published in 1983 by Messrs Darton, Longman & Todd; and to Miss B. L. Hodge at Canterbury for her professional skill in producing the finished typescript from my handwritten MS.

Lingfield 1984   D. W. CLEVERLEY FORD

CONTENTS

INTRODUCTION

This book does not aim at presenting a life of Christ in the form of a collection of sermons. To write such a life is impossible because the materials for it are unavailable. What we possess in the way of resources in the four gospels are *proclamations* of Christ, albeit in story form; they are not biographies. This is not to say they contain no hard facts, but there is fact plus interpretation, not always easy to separate. Nor is it to assert that the gospels do not bring us into contact with the historical Jesus but only into contact with the various writers' impressions of him. Are we to claim that Holbein's portrait of his family painted in 1528/9, and now in the Musée des Beaux-Arts, Basle, only tells us what he thought his wife and family looked like but not what they were really like? The four portraits we have of Jesus painted by the four evangelists, Matthew, Mark, Luke and John – there may be more if we take into account their source material – differ in a number of particulars, but, with the difference, they all present the same recognizable historical man.

No, what this book offers is twenty-six proclamations of Christ in sermon form drawing the material from the proclamation called the four gospels. To use the gospels in this way is to be true to them, for as Form Criticism has demonstrated, even the form of the material provided there has been determined by its employment in the ministry of preaching on the part of the early Church.

Preaching implies a congregation. It implies a congregation meeting in a particular place, at a particular time and with pastoral needs. This has still to be kept in mind when preaching through the life of Christ. The aim is not to reconstruct, if possible, the life story of the Man from Nazareth; nor even to convey an impression of his personality. The aim in preaching is so to present incidents and aspects of his life that twentieth century people may hear some word of God addressed to them now where they are. This is how the ministry of the word is designed to operate, especially at the Eucharist, the sacrament of the real presence of God. The reading of the short passage from the gospels becomes the Gospel for the day, God's good news in the contemporary situation.

There are however defects in hearing only a series of disconnected extracts. What is needed is an awareness of the whole. This the four gospels provide. Contained in them is a developing story with a beginning and an end. I have not therefore presented my twenty-six sermons as a miscellaneous collection based on a random

selection of texts from the four gospels, but arranged them so as to
cover the story of Jesus as it has been presented by the four
evangelists. Obviously I have been obliged to be drastically
selective in order to keep within the agreed extent of this work but I
have tried to maintain a fair balance between incident and teaching,
and between the pastoral needs of individual piety and community
responsibility.

I hope that what I have written may help some to see Jesus
perhaps more vividly, because quite apart from theological
convictions about him he must have been a remarkable man to have
evoked such strong reactions among those who encountered him,
some for, some against. Amazement at Jesus of Nazareth is not
however the sum total of faith in Christ, though it may begin there.
This is the hope of the preacher who preaches through his life.
What is more, faith in Christ must never drift away from the
biblical Jesus. It is as we see Jesus that content is given to the Christ
of faith. The Church has the responsibility laid upon it to keep the
story of Jesus before the eyes of the world. The late Archbishop
Garbett, a wise pastor, used to say that in every parish the story of
Jesus *as a whole* ought to be told at least once every three years.
Perhaps my book will help.

Some of the sermons have been preached, and I have not rubbed
out allusions to those places in the course of them. Others have
been written specially but always with some particular congregation in mind. Preaching to be preaching must always do this.

In an Appendix at the end of the book I have listed the Sundays in
the ASB where the various texts used for the sermons occur in the
Gospel readings for the Eucharist, and some in the lessons for
Evening Prayer. In addition some texts are taken from passages in
the gospels parallel to the Gospel or lesson for the day. A case in
point is Palm Sunday where I have chosen to preach from the
Johannine version of that event. It is not however the main function
of this book to provide comments on the ASB readings. Such is the
aim of other books in this series which I edit. Nevertheless if the list
of references helps to spark off ideas for particular Sundays it will
not be altogether out of place.

D.W.C.F.

1. To the Rescue Came

Matthew 1.23 *God is with us.*

I don't suppose more than a handful of people knew or even troubled to enquire about the actual room or bed in which Sir Winston Churchill was born; or for that matter Joseph Stalin or Franklin Delano Roosevelt. I doubt whether more than a dozen people concerned themselves with the cradle wherein John Wesley was rocked, or how Luther's mother fed her child Martin, or when Augustine first saw the light of day *until* – yes, that is the significant word *until* – they became famous. Then everybody wanted to know. Everybody had questions to put about each one of them. Where was he born? What sort of people were his parents? Was there any sign at the outset of his forthcoming greatness? And answers would be provided. They would have to be.

1. Christmas impossible until . . .

So it was with Jesus of Nazareth. There was no urgency to enquire where he was cradled beyond the immediate family who knew it anyway *until* he became famous. When as a boy he was playing in the narrow streets of Nazareth with a hoop or a top (or whatever were the toys then) no one was inclined to investigate his origins. And when as a grown man he was working as a carpenter or giving a hand in the harvest fields as everyone did, no one asked about the cot in which his mother laid him. Why should they? And when even as a preacher he startled his townsfolk in Nazareth and eyebrows were raised, it was only to remark, 'Where does he get it all from? His family is nothing in particular.' What is more, when at the last Jesus stood as a prisoner before Caiaphas and Pontius Pilate no one pleaded his case on the grounds that his birth was miraculous, or that shepherds recognized his identity, or that oriental kings came to acknowledge him bearing their gifts. No, the Christmas stories, even the actual designation 'Christmas day' were quite impossible *until* something happened to make him famous. And that something was his crucifixion and subsequent resurrection.

2. Christmas certain

That crucifixion and resurrection really were epoch-making. How different everything was after them. How different when the once

1

self-effacing apostles were actually seen and heard publicly proclaiming Jesus of Nazareth as the Christ! How different when
hundreds and hundreds of men and women, yes and even some
Jewish priests, began assembling on the first day of each week to
worship Jesus as Lord! How different when Saul of Tarsus, now
become Paul a Christian, traversing a significant part of the Roman
Empire founded Gentile Churches in major cities! And how about
the fact that in 1950 in Africa nearly 2,000 years later, there were
twenty-five million worshippers of Christ, and by 1975 one hundred million? Is it really surprising that people should want to
know how it all started? What is there about Jesus of Nazareth that
produces such consequences? Where did he come from? To what
level of culture and education did his home belong? After all, it isn't
as if his public career was lengthy. Only three years if that, less than
a normal American presidency or English parliamentary term. And
who could call backwater Galilee and Judaea in AD29 a *public* stage?
So the insistent question. *How could* a man become famous in such a
time and in such a place? But that he did makes Christmas certain.
People were bound to ask how it all began. They were certain to
leave no stone unturned to discover something, at least something
about his birthday and to proclaim it with interpretations and
trumpets.

3. The aim of the Christmas stories

So we in our day celebrate the birthday of Jesus with all the
festivities, music and decoration of which we are capable but not
because he was born of a virgin, or was recognized by shepherds
from the fields, or was sought out by oriental kings bearing their
gifts. We celebrate the birthday of Jesus on account of the reason
for which he became famous. We celebrate it because as time went
on it became clear that in him God dwelt in a unique fashion, so
dwelt in him, so uniquely dwelt in him, that a great leap of faith was
intellectually justified and the conviction maintained that no less a
title was adequate for him than 'Son of God', and he, this 'Son of
God', actually grew up in our world and walked its streets and
lanes. This is the explanation of Christmas.

Oh, I know it takes some believing! I know all this belongs to a
different level of thinking than that with which we are normally
preoccupied – rates, taxes, tariff barriers, mortgages and productiv-
ity agreements. Here we have to come to terms with concepts like

mystery, miracle and the nature of being itself. The gospel writers Matthew and Luke had to face these ultimate questions when they came to write the stories of Jesus's origins. Because of who they believed he was they could not produce an account like an entry in *Who's Who*. They felt bound by their faith to write the story of his earliest years with symbolic interpretation woven in, and the weaving was so close it is now impossible to tear it apart without destroying the whole. In St Matthew, chapters 1 and 2, and St Luke, chapters 1 and 2, we are therefore dealing with poetry because we are dealing with profundities about life which cannot be caught with words in any other way than by poetic symbolism albeit with an historical substratum.

Is this way of reading the Christmas stories disturbing? But I am out to save them from being a stumbling block for adults. All too readily we moderns conditioned by scientific approaches rank them as appropriate, maybe, for the uncritical stage of childhood and appropriate, maybe, for the two or three days at this festive season when we all profit by becoming a bit childlike, if not childish; but for rational men and women they can act as a hindrance to faith, and faith is what we desperately need today. If however we turn ourselves round and see why they were written – not to present a biography of Jesus but to proclaim his identity – they will be acceptable, no, more than acceptable, they will tell us why it is right to worship the *infant* Christ. He did not become the Son of God, he was all along the Son of God, more than that, the Son of God come for our rescue.

4. The Christmas gospel

Here then in these stories lies the Christmas gospel, the Christmas good news. Christ is come as our rescuer from helplessness. 'God is with us.'

Let me tell you a story. It comes from a pastor in Germany. He describes how he found himself in a cellar in one of Germany's major cities. It proved to be a meeting place for drug addicts. He was not wearing clerical dress but a brightly coloured shirt. As he entered someone called out 'Hi, what do you want here?' 'Don't worry', he replied, 'it's all right.' So a girl standing next to him burst out laughing and handed him some hashish. When he declined it they were alerted. 'Why not?' they urged; and when he replied, 'I've lost the taste', they became suspicious. 'Hey, who are you?' 'I'll give you one guess', he countered. A young woman jumped in. 'A butcher', she suggested. 'Wrong', he answered, 'I am a clergyman.' Immediately the whole place was stung into silence. Then they began to talk. They talked till they got round to life's deepest questions and what was the point of it all. At first the pastor found himself with a tough battle on his hands. Before he left, however, he was conscious of the presence of Christ in the midst who prayed 'Father, forgive them for they know not what they do'. He sat there with them until two o'clock in the morning. He even prayed for them, there in the cellar. And some of them prayed with him too. It was a genuine cry to the crucified and risen Christ to rescue them from the helplessness into which they had fallen.

Our world is caught in a many-sided helplessness. We solve one problem only to slide into another, and as our optimistic schemes for betterment grow tarnished with recurring disappointments disillusionment takes over. And then we stop believing in anyone any more or in anything any more. And when hopelessness gets a hold helplessness is not far behind. Even prosperity lags. Some try to meet the situation with any narcotic available – work, pleasure, alcohol, hashish. Why not? Let us eat and drink for tomorrow the nuclear bombs. Who knows? What we desperately need is rescue from helplessness, rescue from hopelessness, rescue by means of the lifeline of faith, reasonable faith, faith in the Christ we proclaim at Christmas, the Christ who came to our world for our rescue. And see how he came to it. See how the gospel tells us he came to it. In poverty, in humility, with the threat of annihilation poised over his head, pushed around by scheming major powers, a refugee on the road. The Lord of all among the little people, you might even think he was one of the little people, just like the shepherds in the fields keeping watch over their flocks by night. But he wasn't one of the little people. He had a major work to do at Golgotha for us men and our rescue. He was born to do it. This is the gospel of Christmas day. This is what the stories about him proclaim. 'God is with us.'

So let us sing our carols with fervency and with understanding. Let our voices express what we believe in our hearts – faith in our divine/human rescuer, for it is by this means we shall be rescued. This is the miracle of Jesus.

2. Jesus is Different

Luke 2.44, 45 (RSV) . . . *they sought him among their kins-folk and acquaintances, and when they did not find him, they returned to Jerusalem seeking him.*

On 19 December 1982 a twelve-year-old boy called Richard Drew went with a friend to a nearby house to pluck a turkey and earn some pocket money. It was early evening. Since he had not returned at the expected time his parents grew anxious, as well they might. He never did arrive. On the way back he was set on by a man jumping out of the bushes who knifed him. Frogmen found his body some days later in a water-filled gravel pit. A terrible story.

1. Jesus gets lost

Each year at Epiphanytide it is customary to hear again the story of another twelve-year-old boy who got lost; but the occasion was nothing like as macabre as that already described, though it could have been. Knifing boys was not invented yesterday. His parents, nevertheless, were scared out of their wits. Torn with anxiety they went searching for him, but they went to the wrong place. This is the sharp point of my text and indeed of the incident as described. '. . . they sought him among their kinsfolk and acquaintances, and when they did not find him, they returned to Jerusalem seeking him.'

The story of course is about the boy Jesus taken by his parents on his first visit to Jerusalem for the Passover festival. Crowds of people made this annual pilgrimage together turning it into a kind of religious outing much enjoyed by all, not least twelve-year-olds seeing their fantastic capital for the first time. I do not think however that St Luke recorded this incident with the same motive as did the reporter telling of Richard Drew on 19 December. He was out to use this story about Jesus as an instrument for showing how different he was, different at twelve, different from the start. And if we do not recognize this we shall look for him in the wrong place, and then we shall not find him.

2. Jesus gets found

The mistake Jesus's parents made was that they took it for granted

that their son would be in the pilgrimage party among their kins-
folk and acquaintances. Do not blame them. Where would you
expect a twelve-year-old to be but with those of his own age? And
that Joseph and Mary did take this for granted shows how ordinary
and normal (superficially anyway) Jesus appeared to those who
knew him best. But they were wrong. They had not 'taken in' that
this boy was different.

What happened was this. The pilgrim party in a body started for
home, the festival over, down the dangerous Jerusalem–Jericho
road, dangerous on account of the robbers lurking in the hills. At
the end of the day Joseph and Mary looked for Jesus. Normally
families would be together at night. But Jesus was missing. Did the
parents sleep at all that night? Would you? Next morning, we may
guess, at first light they toiled up that wearisome road again, back
to Jerusalem. And in that city what doors they must have knocked
on, enquiring with fear mounting more frighteningly as they
received negative after negative reply to their urgent question,
'Have you seen a twelve-year-old boy up from Galilee?' And after
three hideously dark days they thought of the temple. And there he
was. Utterly absorbed in the theological discussions he found in
progress there, not only listening but actually putting questions,
index of his alert and enquiring mind.

(a) Jesus found and lost

How did a twelve-year-old survive three days in Jerusalem alone?
Where did he sleep? Who fed him? Did some kind woman put him
up? Who was she? St Luke tells us nothing about these matters. All
he says is that Jesus's parents were astonished to find him in the
temple; but even more astonished that he seemed so unconcerned
about them. Mary his mother felt deeply hurt. 'Son, why have you
treated us so? Behold, your father and I have been looking for you
anxiously' (that was putting it mildly!). But there was more hurt
to come. 'How is it that you sought me? Did you not know I must
be in my Father's house?' Apparently not. And so Jesus seemed
be a stranger. In one sense they had found him, but in another sense
they suddenly felt they had lost him. Joseph and Mary indeed were
not the first parents nor the last to undergo the experience of half
losing their growing children, but with them it was puzzling as
well as hurting. 'They did not understand the saying which he
spoke to them', is St Luke's poignant comment. But Jesus did not

leave them. He resumed the trek back to Nazareth, an undistinguished place, and lived the undistinguished life his undistinguished parents provided for him, but Mary was more than a little puzzled.

Thus St Luke warns us with this story that in the narrative he is about to provide we shall encounter a man we shall never wholly understand. True, he was in a way like other boys at the age of twelve but even then he was different. He lived his life as a man like others of his time – in clothing, in food, in life style and thought forms. Yet he was different. And if we are unprepared at the outset to see him as different – St Luke would say *essentially* different and not simply different as all humans are from one another – we shall lose him, indeed, we shall never find him as he really is. This is what St Luke would have us grasp. Jesus was different.

(b) The wrong place

I think many of us are like Joseph and Mary, so familiar in a way with Jesus by reason of our education and upbringing that we have never really grasped how different he was. And so we go looking for him in the wrong place. We think of him as one among the founders of great religions – Moses, Confucius, Buddha, Mohammed. Because of the so-called multiracial and multireligious character of Britain this is becoming commonplace thinking. Take your pick. It doesn't much matter which you choose; they are all much alike. Are they? The story St Luke includes in Chapter 2 of his gospel cries aloud that Jesus was different and that we shall never find him if we go looking in the wrong place, that is among these other religious leaders, notwithstanding the undoubted truths to which their religious systems testify.

3. Jesus is different

Jesus was different. Let Hans Küng in his book *On Being a Christian* tell us how different. Jesus was not reared in a court like Moses, nor was he a king's son like Buddha. He was not a scholar and politician like Confucius, nor a rich merchant like Mohammed. The fact that his origin was so insignificant makes his enduring significance all the more amazing.

But this obscure origin pales before what follows. He did not fit any known category of leader and never has. He belonged neither to the ruling class nor to the rebels against the ruling class. He was no moralist like the Pharisees nor an ascetic like the Essenes. He supported no political party and certainly no political party supported him. He was not a trained scholar, yet in dialectical skill he was more than a match for any. He was not a priest, and if he might be categorized as a prophet he was unlike any prophet before or since. He set up no organization, not even a Church.

And when his death is taken into account its manner is incomparable. Let Hans Küng speak again: 'Moses died in the midst of his people at the age of one hundred and twenty "his eyes undimmed and his vigour unfaded". Buddha at eighty peacefully, his disciples around him. Confucius returned in old age to Lu where he edited the ancient writings of his people. Mohammed, after he had thoroughly enjoyed the last years of his life as political ruler of Arabia, died in the midst of his harem in the arms of his favourite wife.' Jesus however was tortured to death through a miscarriage of justice, forsaken by his followers, even it seemed by God, and he was only thirty-three. Whichever way you look at Jesus he was different. There has been, there is, no one like him.

St Luke tells us that we shall have to start from the fact that Jesus was different if ever we are to grasp his real significance. Not that we shall ever wholly understand him and certainly not claim him. Joseph and Mary came to know that he was apart from them and they from him. Yet they trusted him. Is not this what we must do? Is not this trust the essence of the Christian religion? And if dark days come to us, as they may, times and circumstances when we do not understand what God is doing to us, even as Mary said 'Son, why have you treated us so?', if some tragedy or illness or breakdown causes doubts, even resentment to arise, and maybe part if not the whole of the Christian creed seems to make little sense – still we must trust Christ because there is no one else in the world like him nor ever has been. Jesus was different. I dare to say he was unique. In the last resort it is there that the power of the Christian gospel resides. Do not look in the wrong place.

3. Equipped for Ministry

Mark 1.11 (NEB) *And a voice spoke from heaven: 'Thou art my Son, my Beloved; on thee my favour rests.'*

A little time ago I was told of a young mother who suddenly

realized that somewhere in the house her three small daughters were unnaturally quiet. Slightly alarmed, she went searching for them. And there they were, 'glued' to the television having surreptiously found out that there was to be a programme entitled 'Birth of a baby'.

1. The totality of birth

At various levels of understanding we never cease to be fascinated by the whole idea of human birth. In his book *Smouldering Fire* Dr Martin Israel reminds us how the birth of a person is a *comprehensive* event. First there is physical birth when the child begins a separate existence from its mother. But this is not all. There comes the time when the growing child makes independent decisions with a mind and will of its own. So individuality is born. Thereafter there is a distinct personality with marked characteristics, temperament and potentiality for achievements, the focus of all of which is the soul or psyche. There may be a third stage not experienced by all, this is spiritual birth when the individual opens to the Spirit of God. Spiritual identity is then discovered, but not only that, there is also an awareness of a new power and authority beyond that of the soul itself.

Jesus experienced all three stages of birth. There was the primary event we celebrate at Christmas, with our representation of the baby in a manger and Mary his mother sitting by, a theme for a host of the world's greatest painters. As with every child, so the child Jesus was wholly dependent for some time on his mother. She fed him, she washed him, she dressed him; above all she loved him. Would he have become the man above all others had she not dandled him, cuddled him and cooed to him? I think not. There cannot be rounded development in the absence of love from the start.

But he had to break away. For individuality to be born there has to be independent action operating through the mind and will, painful to both parents and child. Birth always involves pain. St Luke who gives us in his gospel a picture of Mary giving birth also tells us how that son, now twelve years old, began to break away from his parents. They 'lost' him because he stayed behind in the Temple when the pilgrim party, including his parents, had begun to move off home to Galilee. The hurt for the parents was not only the event of losing him but the awareness that they were losing him *mentally*. They could not understand him altogether. He was moving away from them. His individuality now born was being developed. It went on developing all through his 'teens and twenties. It developed when, as is likely, he faced the loss of his father and when he became the standby of his widowed mother. It developed when he had to act as father to the younger members of the household, and when he ran the small carpentry business for which his father had been responsible. And through all these hurting experiences and responsibilities he watched people and listened to people. He also drank deeply of the beauty of the countryside round about his home town Nazareth, and saw how people reacted to the pains and pleasures of life. All this coupled with prayer and a keen intelligence caused the birth of a personality, a psyche quite outstanding in its own human-ness. Those who knew him in Nazareth must have wondered what would become of him.

What did come is best set down in St Mark's own words 'It happened at the time that Jesus came from Nazareth in Galilee and was baptized in the Jordan by John. At the moment when he came out of the water, he saw the heavens torn open and the spirit like a dove descending upon him. And a voice spoke from heaven: "Thou art my Son, my Beloved, on thee my favour rests."' This event is recorded in all four gospels. It is one of the five great events of his life, the others being his birth, his transfiguration, his crucifixion and his resurrection. It represents his birth in the Spirit, the third stage of the totality of birth which he experienced. From then on he was conscious of being the Son of God.

2. *The overriding requirement for the ministry*

And then it happened. After Jesus had experienced the totality of birth, all three stages, he began his public ministry, so short, and yet so significant for the whole world.

There is a story in the second chapter of the book called Exodus in the Old Testament, which tells of the young man Moses consumed with a passion to deliver his fellow countrymen from the degrading and dehumanizing conditions of slavery they were suffering in Egypt at the hands of Pharaoh Rameses II. And there came a day when he set about making a start on the deliverance he knew to be so urgent. He struck down an Egyptian who was beating a Hebrew and buried the corpse in the sand. Next day he attempted to intervene in a quarrel between two Hebrews but when one of them enquired with a sneer if he was about to commit murder as he had done the previous day, Moses saw that he would be well advised to flee for his life. The truth was he had to wait for the *spiritual experience*, commonly called the Burning Bush (Exodus 3) before he could offer leadership to his oppressed people.

Jesus, no doubt also burning to lead, made no such mistake. We hear nothing of him before his anointing by the Spirit at the river Jordan, nothing about alleviating people in pain, nothing about guiding them with his undoubted wisdom. Are we then to suppose that he was unsure of people's needs? Are we to suppose that he was not already in himself a man of superior qualities of body and mind, a wholly integrated personality capable of great achievements? But he did nothing in the way of a public ministry until he was born in the Spirit and knew for a certainty his identity. 'Thou art my Son, my Beloved; on thee my favour rests.'

3. The experience of birth in the Spirit

It would be profitable to look at the constituent parts of this experience of birth in the Spirit. There were three. First there was the closing of the door, on the part of Jesus to his old life. Not that it was a bad life in any respect, but it was a life in which the skills and accomplishments were the product of his own authentic and integrated personality, in no way to be despised or underrated. An integrated personality is the sure ground on which great work is accomplished by the great in all ages. But there was more. There was in the second place an identification with the people to whom and on behalf of whom he was to minister, an identification publicly symbolized by the ritual act of baptism in the Jordan river. Then thirdly there was the Word of God addressed to him personally establishing his unique identity. 'Thou art my Son, my Beloved; on thee my favour rests.' So the Spirit of God descended on him and in communion with that Spirit his own spirit pulsated with the divine life and energy. Then he was ready for service, and how swiftly and decisively he moved. St Mark of all the evangelists catches the tempo.

4. The message for us

The question may well be asked what message if any, this experi-

ence of Jesus of Nazareth has for us? We are not the Christ. We
have not his distinctive ministry.

It has a message for the Church, which is his body and which is
called to proclaim him and to minister in his name. It serves as a
reminder that for all the undoubted wisdom, expertise and scholarship collectively possessed by the Church, evident not least in the
General Synods, publications, cultural and charitable works, without the Spirit of God little of what God requires of it will be
achieved. And if it stands aloof from the people in some misguided
stance of moral superiority it will not reach them with the Gospel.
Identification with those to whom the ministry is carried out is
essential. Then, when the Spirit of God is received, things begin to
happen. The disciples of Christ found this out in the upper room in
Jerusalem that first Whitsunday.

There is also a message for the individual. For all the unquestionable value of a secure home and a good mother (it is interesting
how much a number of outstanding leaders have confessed they
owe to their mothers), and for all the unquestionable excellence of
the heights to which the human mind and soul can rise when the
whole personality is integrated, even so it is true that the full stature
and potentiality of man is not reached until he recognizes his
identity as a son of God, and is open to the energizing Spirit of
God. This is an explanation of why the really great *are* great and
achieve so much; but there is a word here as well for the rest of us.
We shall be surprised what we can do if we rely less on our own
strength and more on the energy which God gives to all who are
open to him. The prophet Zechariah put this in a nutshell many
centuries ago. 'Not by might, nor by power, but by my spirit, saith
the Lord' (Zechariah 4.6).

4. Jesus Tempted

Mark 1.12, 13 (RSV) *The Spirit immediately drove him out
into the wilderness. And he was in the wilderness forty days,
tempted by Satan.*

1. Led into temptation

This is an odd statement for St Mark to make that Jesus was driven
by the Spirit out into the wilderness to be tempted by Satan. Had

he written that Jesus was driven *by Satan* out into the wilderness it would surely have accorded more with our notions. But this is not what St Mark tells us. He says *the Spirit* drove Jesus into temptation. All of which is on a par with this phrase in the Lord's prayer which troubles so many sincere people – 'Lead us not into temptation'. Just as if God would! But apparently he does. At least he led Jesus into temptation right there in the wilderness close to the baptismal site at the Jordan river; and the word 'led' is insufficiently strong. The Greek word means 'thrust out', even 'thrown out'. It was a terrible ordeal Jesus underwent in the wilderness, terrible because breaking under it was so likely, so easy. Most people could not stand this degree of testing; which no doubt is why our Lord invited us to beseech God not to lead *us* into temptation. We most certainly would break.

2. Jesus's temptations

But what about Jesus being tempted at all? The letter to the Hebrews in the New Testament categorically asserts that Jesus is 'one who in every respect has been tempted as we are, yet without sin' (4.15). Very well, let the point be taken. He was tempted but he did not sin. It is one thing to be tempted. It is quite another thing to succumb to the temptation. And if the tempted one does not succumb, a victory has been won, a stiffening of character is the outcome and a consequent increase in moral stature. Temptation is not sin.

Nevertheless the question will not go away. *With what* was Jesus tempted? Was he tempted to get drunk? Certainly not in the wilderness. There were no pubs there! Forget the forty days' sojourn for a moment. Was he ever tempted to go running after the easy girls in, say, nearby Tiberias down by the lake? or when they made eyes at him in, say, Capernaum? Remember he was a strong upstanding male. Did he have to fight with himself in his teens not to go sniffing glue or whatever was the narcotic in vogue in his day, because we can be sure drugs were available. The merchants from Damascus and beyond crossing Galilee on their way to Acre did not only carry gold, frankincense and myrrh! Are these suggestions shocking? But we have to face it. The writer of the letter to the Hebrews does say he was '*in every respect tempted as we are*'! One theologian, I observe, declares that Jesus had to be tempted with all the world's sins if he was to bear away all the world's sins.

I do not think he was tempted in these ways at all. A person's temptations are an indication of that person's quality. A sensitive aesthetic type will not be tempted with the coarse. A coarse, vulgar, loud-mouthed type will not be tempted with the refined. We can be certain the devil knew perfectly well where Jesus was *not* vulnerable. He wasn't going to waste his weapons fighting on the pitch of crude instincts where he knew he could not possibly win with Jesus.

And know this. If the devil knew what a phoney war it would be trying to do battle with Jesus by tempting him with sensuality the divine Spirit knew it even better. There would not even be any temptation. So he did not drive him down to Tiberias, the heathen city where the world, the flesh and the devil were making hay, he drove him into the wilderness where there was not even anything to act as a reminder of the sensual. But there was loneliness, day after day and night after night. There was the deadly peril of prolonged introspection. There was the weakening of the mind and of the will through the progressive debilitating of the flesh. There was the strong possibility even probability, of doubt as to whether God cares if we live or die, or of what use it is to know that one is, in any sense, a Son of God.

3. Strong points

Think of this. The temptations of Jesus assailed him at his *strong* points. They hit him hard when he knew for a surety that stupendous powers lay within them; they came on like a flood when he was conscious of his special relationship to God, so close that it was like a Father-Son relationship. Jesus was tempted when he saw the whole panorama of his foreordained ministry stretching out before him and the public stage he knew he was about to mount, having shut the carpenter's shop down in Nazareth and left it behind him for ever. He was tempted when he knew in his bones what he could do with people. So his self-authenticating personal power dictated the testing place for his battle with the devil. And it was fierce. He had to win. He could not be the Christ if he failed there.

I have read recently that the temptation for Jesus was self-aggrandizement. I do not believe it. I see Jesus come from his baptism in the Jordan river full of the spirit of dedication to minister *on behalf of the common people*. He saw them wistfully longing for something better in life than endless drudgery, uncertainty and sordidness, which is why they flocked down to the river Jordan to get baptized by John in some kind of religious revival they only half understood, and which did not mature. So closely did Jesus identify with them in their hopelessness and helplessness, though anything but hopeless and helpless himself, that he even got baptized too. It was this ministry to people that filled his mind when he was driven by the Spirit to be tempted in the wilderness. It was his own powers which he could use in this ministry that dominated his whole consciousness then. Not self-aggrandizement. There was temptation but his temptation struck at *the way* in which he would use this power with people. His temptation was to obtain quick results, to adopt dazzling methods and to follow the world's way of wielding force for the supposed benefit of people.

St Matthew and St Luke spell this out in story form. They tell of a temptation in the wilderness to turn stones into bread. How in crowds the world's starving would come flocking to his feet if a food programme is what he could lay on. Then they would listen to the things of the spirit. But would they? Next the temptation to dazzle people's love of the stupendous. Jump off the temple parapet and walk away unharmed! No need to get people to think. The majority can't think anyway. So be a wizard of a leader. It would assemble a congregation in no time. And then the temptation to fiddle, to compromise, to delude the masses even a little. Do not all leaders of all great movements act this way? Is it not necessary? After all the public is foolish. It does not know what is for its good! How then could he, Jesus, fail if, with all his latent powers he worked along these lines?

But he resisted. With nothing more than the word of God proclaimed through the Scriptures available to all, he hit back at the tempter who (we may guess in anger) bolted from the field of battle. Jesus won. He won that day. And if he had to fight again another day he won and won again. Had he not done so the world would never have seen him pinned to a Roman cross!

4. Our temptations

What about our temptations? We must be very far gone in spiritual insensitivity if we reckon that none of this applies in our case. And we must be at a very elementary stage in our understanding of human nature if we reckon that temptations only strike at our weak points, though of course they do strike there. And we need to be aware of the fact that apparently strong men not infrequently have weak points unsuspected by the admiring public but not by the disbelieving devil. To how many of the thousands of viewers who watched the 1983 BBC TV production, *The Life and Times of Lloyd George*, the man who did so much for Britain during the Great War, did it come as a shock to learn that over and over again he was made a fool of by a woman with a pretty face? And every now and then the newspapers make revelations of some respectable public figure who is shown to have a secret pile of pornographic pictures tucked away in a drawer for private viewing. And disappointed men in public life take to the bottle. And women run through fortunes in dress. All these are weak points.

But we also get tested at our strong points. A man with a double first from Oxbridge is tempted to become an intellectual snob. A woman with an impeccable pedigree will invite no one to her house who is not listed in Burke's. A brilliant company manager will not even talk to a member of his work force. A medallist in athletics reckons everyone without ball-sense a poor fool. Yes, and the cathedral worshipper is tempted to smile pityingly at the Salvation Army band, and the Pentecostalist at the poor, stuffed, stiff Anglican Mattins-goer. Be sure the devil will be working overtime in all these characters.

What are the weapons for resisting – providing, that is, we see the need to resist and have the will to resist? First, to be forewarned is to be forearmed. We need to know the weak points and the strong points in our defences. Secondly, we need the guide lines which a knowledge of the Scriptures provides showing us what we ought and ought not to do. Thirdly – and let them not be despised – we need the protection of public opinion and the protection of Christian standards, lest we climb fences not to anyone's advantage.

Jesus was tempted and was not beaten. We shall be tempted, and on occasions we shall certainly be beaten. But the Lord Christ knows what the battle is like. He will forgive our sins if we confess them. And tomorrow we shall be able to start again as better men and women.

5. Not to be Written Off

John 1.46 (NEB) *'Nazareth!' Nathaniel exclaimed; 'can anything good come from Nazareth?'*

Well, that was Nathaniel's idea. I don't know if many others took such a disparaging view of the place, certainly not those who lived there. Perhaps Nathaniel was a snob. Perhaps he was that worst kind of snob, a religious snob. Perhaps he was so closed in on his own way of life that he could not even think how anyone could possibly attain to any form of greatness outside of it. There are people like that. He changed his mind of course in a flash when he met Jesus, but that was the base from which it looks as if he started – cultural and religious snobbery.

1. *An ordinary place*

Nazareth was ordinary, but so were almost all the towns and villages in Judaea and Galilee. The Jews have never excelled in architecture. Nazareth was at least a town and not a village or hamlet, though like all ancient towns it was small. The whole of it would easily fit into Trafalgar Square in London; and since it lacked Greek or Roman influence its streets would be little more than winding alleyways.

Most of the houses built of daub and wattle, easily broken through by thieves, would consist of one room only. Here the whole family lived, ate and slept, except in the hot summer when they transferred to the flat roof when dusk brought the cooler air. The bed was a mat on the floor, the pillow a block of wood or a stone. There was no undressing. Those who possessed a cloak would pull it over them. The cooking was done on the floor outside in a little hollow between two bricks, or under a lean-to when it rained.

Some superior houses did exist. A few boasted two rooms, an upper and a lower. A tiny minority even had several rooms built around a central courtyard. There were some well-to-do land owners who lived in style. Amenities had been learned from the Greek and Roman invaders but it is unlikely that Nazareth enjoyed any. Nazareth was working-class, situated seventy-one miles north of the capital.

This is where Jesus was brought up, no doubt in one of those one-roomed houses up some dingy alleyway. At least nine people occupied it, including Jesus. Privacy was non-existent. Not that a humble background is all that rare among those who have achieved fame. History is littered with instances. Who would have thought that that tiny back-street house in Lossiemouth of all places would have produced a Prime Minister? or that grocer's shop in Grantham? We had better be wary about snobbery over origin and pedigrees, especially if we follow Jesus of Nazareth.

2. A commanding situation

We need to be careful however not to make the assumption that Jesus grew up tucked away in some peasant environment cut off from all contact with the great world outside and was therefore 'green'. In some ways Nazareth was a perfect situation for an alert boy in which to develop. As soon as you left the town, nestling in its little basin in the hills, there lay before you one of the finest panoramas in the whole country. To the West the glazed blue of the Mediterranean Sea and to the East, the stark range of the hills of Gilead. Up there you felt on top of the world. Thirty miles, no less, in three directions you could see. And down there the impressive plain of Esdraelon, site of twenty decisive battles at least. Barak had fought there, and Gideon and more recently the Maccabees. The whole place reeked with history. What a grandstand for a boy!

And not only history. Across the plain there stretched the highway up from the South, from Egypt and Jerusalem, never without its merchants going up and down. And another road plainly visible with caravans wending their way South from Damascus crammed with goods. Then North, the highway connecting Acre on the coast and the Gentile territory east of Galilee. The Roman legions swung in orderly fashion along this and oriental princes with their retinues and their stylish ladies flaunting their wealth. All the 'goings on' in the Roman Empire buzzed in rumour along those busy roads – the state of the Emperor's health, impending political changes in Rome, the scandals Herod was 'up to'. All this filtered into the boy Jesus's ears. And the shocked Jewish talk of the shocking ways in which the Gentiles in Decapolis lived and their hopelessness in face of death. The boys in Nazareth talked over all they heard, and the temptations of the alluring world on their doorstep in no way passed by the exceptional boy in their midst. Jesus was not green. He couldn't be. He was brought up in Nazareth.

3. A good home

'Nazareth!' Nathaniel exclaimed; 'can any good come from Nazareth?' Not perhaps if there were not even one good home in the place. Not perhaps if you can't have a good home without indoor sanitation, electric light and a gas or electric cooker. But suppose there is one stable home, a home where the parents do not even quarrel, let alone break up or bash the babies; suppose up one of those alleyways there exists, even after tragedy has hit it and the breadwinner has died, a home where unfaith and bitterness have not in consequence taken over eating up the maternal love that once made every member of the family feel significant; suppose there is a home there where the mother is a woman of character and of love, and of discipline – is it possible then that out of Nazareth and Nazareth's environment good will come? and not only good but actually some great one? No, it is not just possible. It happened. Out of Nazareth came Jesus whom we call *salvator-mundi*, the saviour of the world. Rightly did Philip reply to Nathaniel's snobby rhetorical question – 'Nazareth! can any good come from Nazareth?', when he said 'Come and see'. That is what we all ought to do, sooner or later, and the sooner the better. See Jesus of Nazareth for ourselves without prejudice.

4. The man himself

What do we see? What did Nathaniel see? He saw a man who looked you straight in the eye, a man in commonplace clothes but with no commonplace stamp. He carried himself with authority and poise. Jesus was not someone with whom you were disposed to take liberties. He lacked any suggestion of inferiority. There was a kind of royalty about him but he exuded no patronage. A man wholly integrated, from which position of personal security and authenticity he read you the moment he saw you. Philip had said to Nathaniel 'Come and see', as if Nathaniel could examine Jesus like an object and express a consequent opinion. But it did not work that way at all. It never did. No one managed to examine Jesus. Instead you felt he was examining you. While Nathaniel was still approaching, Jesus said, 'Here is an Israelite worthy of the name. There is nothing false in him.' Nathaniel was taken aback. 'How do you come to know me?' he asked, mystified. At which moment, I guess, a broad smile covered Jesus's face and his eyes twinkled. 'I saw you under the fig tree before Philip spoke to you.' Nathaniel's breath was quite taken away.

But what about the snobbery? if snobbery it was and not plain scepticism, product of clear observation. 'Nazareth! can any good come from Nazareth?' Had Jesus overheard? or did he simple read snobbery and scepticism in the set of Nathaniel's mouth? Possibly. But the point is that snobbery and scepticism were not all Jesus read there. Never did he see only defects, weaknesses and sins in people. He also recognized potentiality for good. What is more, in his presence, those same people recognized in themselves potentiality for good. That was the extraordinary thing about this man standing in front of you. You wanted to show your best. And yet simultaneously you felt more than a little shabby. Nevertheless, with Jesus the positive not the negative was always uppermost, not what a person is but what the same person could be. This is why the writer of the fourth gospel summed up Jesus's ministry to people by saying that he did not come to condemn but to save. He was out to rescue the best in us and to build on it. We ought to remember this. It is in Christ's presence that we can grow up to our full stature, with a new significance whatever our background, racial, social or moral. It really is surprising what God can bring out of Nazareth and out of people.

6. The Kingdom of God

Mark 1.14, 15 (RSV) *Now after John was arrested, Jesus came into Galilee preaching the gospel of God, and saying 'The time is fulfilled, and the kingdom of God is at hand; repent, and believe the gospel.'*

1. A clear message

In 1983 a large proportion of the British public gave its attention to the manifestos of the main political parties prior to the General Election. They were the cause of unending debate, not only concerning their contents but also who ought to carry the responsibility for drawing them up. Now suppose, just suppose, one party failed to produce a manifesto, or produced one that was so hazy or unpractical as to be unconvincing, is it conceivable that that party would win the election? Any political party, any new movement, must proclaim a clear and concise message.

Now in initiating his ministry in Galilee Jesus was no exception to this. St Mark recording it could scarcely be more explicit. Having completed his prologue in the first thirteen verses of his book (where you would expect the prologue to be) he plunged straight in. 'Let me make clear before we go any further' he wrote in effect, 'what was the overriding message of Jesus's ministry, it was the kingdom of God.' And he might properly have continued 'I shall mention it at least twenty times in my book. This is something of which you, dear reader, must never lose sight. The Kingdom of God is paramount.'

2. Diverse interpretations of the kingdom of God

But what is the kingdom of God? What did Jesus's contemporaries in Galilee and Judaea think it was? What do we think it is?

There was a strong nationalist party based chiefly on Jerusalem, the temple and the law which interpreted it as the kingdom of David, the golden age of the nation's history when the united tribes of Israel were a power to be reckoned with in the Near East.

Then there were the down-to-earth political realists who saw Rome as the source of all the nation's ills. The kingdom of God would come when the secret caches of arms could be opened, the long knives drawn and the hated foreigners be expelled from the land for ever. Freedom fighting! This was the way to bring in the better world.

In addition there were the visionaries. They looked for some gigantic cosmic struggle away in the distant future when the unseen forces of good would wage war on the unseen forces of evil, securing after a mighty cataclysm an era of peace when all people would live in harmony with one another. This would be the kingdom of God.

And we, what do we think at the close of the twentieth century? In so far as we are cognisant with the term 'kingdom of God' at all we suppose it must be another name for Utopia; and half disillusioned as we are with politics, we use it as a synonym for the unobtainable, people being what they are.

3. The kingdom of God is present

Over against all this St Mark tells of a man for whom the kingdom of God was the preoccupation of his life. What is more, he confidently declared it to be at hand, even present in the here and now. This set a problem for his contemporaries. He did not look like a fanatic. He did not sound like a fanatic. Even if that revivalist preacher and moral reformer who immediately preceded him – John Baptist – could conceivably be written off as such, dressed as he was in outlandish clothes and feeding on such meagre provisions as the desert provided where he lived, Jesus could not so be written off. Leading men from Jerusalem felt impelled to journey to provincial Galilee to judge for themselves. What they encountered disturbed them. A man in ordinary, everyday clothes. A man obviously in no sense a recluse, nor an ascetic, nor a political ranter; but a man of extraordinarily powerful personality and commanding presence, a man with more than a hint of royalty about his bearing in spite of his clothes and work-worn hands. A man aged about thirty, clearly in perfect health, and with a way of talking that gripped the attention immediately. That this strong and intelligent man should be referring constantly to the kingdom of God was disturbing. Was he planning an uprising? Those holding the reins of power in the land dare not ignore him.

But what did he say about the kingdom of God? Did it sound seditious? He taught that the kingdom of God is like a man sowing seed some of which falls on the pathway, some on rocky ground, some among the thistles and some on good ground where it produces a patchy harvest. He said it is like a farmer sowing wholesome seed in his field and his enemy comes and strews it with weed seeds. It is like a tiny grain of mustard seed which grows up into a tree, and also like yeast which leavens bread. There seemed no end to the metaphors he employed to depict the kingdom of God – a treasure hidden in a field, a pearl of very special value, worth selling everything to purchase. It is even like the mixed catch of fish drawn up by a drag-net, some of it worthless. So Matthew collected these seven metaphors in seven parables and set them side by side in chapter 13 of his gospel.

What would the crowds that swarmed to hear Jesus make of them? Or, for that matter, what contribution could the deputations down from Jerusalem report to those anxious authorities who had despatched them to find out? What they did grasp was that somehow the kingdom of God as Jesus understood it was intimately bound up with his own person. Had he not said at the outset of his ministry 'The time is fulfilled, the kingdom of God is *at hand*. Change your minds and believe the good news'? So for the safety's sake of the *status quo* in the land the rulers quietly arrived at one conclusion. To eliminate this enigmatic talk of a kingdom present somewhere, somehow Jesus must be eliminated. Only one question remained open. How?

4. *Jesus's interpretation of the kingdom of God*

But what in truth is the kingdom of God as Jesus understood it? The answer to this question was clearly given when his disciples approached him with a request to be taught how to pray. He said, 'When you pray say, "Our Father who art in heaven, hallowed be thy name"', or, as St Luke has it according to the New English Bible,
> 'Father, thy name be hallowed;
> Thy kingdom come'.

Did the disciples start when they heard of the kingdom once more, the kingdom of God? And did they at last grasp its meaning when they heard him continue as in St Matthew's extended version,
> 'Thy will be done
> On earth as in heaven'?

So this is what the kingdom of God is. Not some form of recovered national superiority; nor the wresting of power from foreign occupation by armed rebellion; nor some apocalyptic vision; and certainly not an unrealizable Utopia. No, the kingdom of God is God's will done on earth as it is in heaven. It is to be experienced in the here and now, but only in patches, gradually and at a price, till it is finally realized in its totality beyond time. But – and this is important for without it there is no Christian gospel – once, and in totality, it actually came into being. God's will *was done* perfectly on earth as it is in heaven. This was the life, death and resurrection of Jesus. In him the kingdom of God was at hand. It was really present. Jesus of Nazareth, come in the fulness of time, is God's kingdom realized. He is the embodiment of the kingdom, the kingdom incarnated. No wonder he is represented in the fourth gospel as testifying before Pilate 'My kingdom is not of this world'. No wonder he had a gospel to proclaim. No wonder the Church has a gospel to proclaim. The kingdom of God *has already come*, in the person of Jesus.

5. *The kingdom of God today*

And where is that kingdom today? Did it die with Jesus? Did it flare up like a beacon only to fade away as suddenly within a space of years? Certainly those who engineered his crucifixion hoped that this would be the case. But is Jesus dead? Is the spirit of Jesus dead? Is not the resurrection of Jesus, the risenness of Jesus a fact of experience for millions upon millions of people? Where is the kingdom of God today?

Let me tell you where the kingdom of God is. In Northern Ireland. Yes, I said Northern Ireland. It is in the thirty organizations and more, and the innumerable street and neighbourhood groups whose members give up their spare time, without money or glory, to repair their ravaged community. It is reflected in those courageous men and women acting alone who for instance keep the shop open during an IRA funeral and refuse to let their children riot on the streets. There are many women who take a hand in this, Christians in the proper sense of the word. Cheerful people, even inclined to laugh at their problems. A recurring theme among them is forgiveness. There is Hylda Armstrong, a widow in constant pain from a car accident. When her peace-worker son, Sean, was murdered by an unknown gunman, instead of withdrawing in bitterness, she helped to set up the Harmony Trust, providing a home for seaside holidays for Catholic and Protestant children together. Since 1975 many more than four thousand have profited by it. And there is Father Regan, RUC detective Ben Forde, factory worker Nellie Morgan, and dentist Cecilia Lineham. The kindness, generosity, forgiveness and self-sacrificing care of people shown by these and many others is astonishing. No, not astonishing. It is the kingdom of God realized in our time in war-torn Northern Ireland.

What is the secret of the kingdom of God? Can there be any doubt? It is Jesus Christ himself. Whenever men and women put their faith in him, caring, forgiving, self-sacrificing relationships begin to blossom in the community. So God's will is done on earth as it is in heaven. It is to this end that we go on proclaiming the Christian gospel. It is what the Church is for.

7. Jesus the Synagogue Preacher

Luke 4.21 (NEB)   *He began to speak: 'Today', he said 'in your very hearing this text has come true.'*

I wish I could do that. I wish all our preachers could do that – take up the Old Testament, take up the New Testament, and so expose it that it *comes* true to the hearers there and then. I wonder how Jesus did it? I wonder because the congregation in the Nazareth synagogue where he was preaching certainly possessed no inclination whatsoever to recognize him as fulfilling in his person the prophesies of their scriptures. How then, when they saw those musty old scripture scrolls exhibited once again that Sabbath, as they must have seen a hundred times, how was it they were not bored to tears when they saw the Chazzan hand him the scroll of the prophet Isaiah to read? – What that again? . . . Perhaps you know the feeling!

1. The preacher himself

First, I think there must have been something about the preacher himself that arrested their attention. I observe that St Luke introduces this preaching event with the words 'reports about him spread through the whole countryside. He taught in their synagogues and all men sang his praises.' So apparently Jesus came to Nazareth with a reputation as a preacher. This helps. People listen if they expect something.

And then St Luke makes this point. After Jesus had opened the scroll, found the text, read it, re-rolled the scroll, returned it to the Chazzan and sat down – yes, St Luke records all these details of actions, which must have been deliberate and taken time – 'all eyes', he says, 'in the synagogue were fixed *on him*'.

I repeat there must have been something about the preacher, something beyond the curiosity of the older members of the congregation who remembered Jesus as a boy in Nazareth playing with a hoop (or whatever were the toys in those days). My wife can remember how when she was a small girl she saw a little boy called Eric Abbott playing with a top in the street outside his home. He whipped it vigorously. That memory, however, is not the sole reason, if much of a reason at all, why she listened to him when he became Dean of Westminster. I say again there was something about Jesus as a preacher that made you look, as well as listen, whenever he spoke.

I have no doubt Jesus 'blossomed through his mouth', to employ George Adam Smith's comment on the opening words of the second Servant Song, in Isaiah 49. All the graciousness, incisiveness and depth of his personality came out *in his voice*. Not surprisingly then, St Luke makes this further comment on the immediate effect of Jesus's preaching, 'they were surprised that words of such grace should proceed from his lips'. I cannot think that this refers only to content (though I know how striking it is that he left out the bit about the day of vengeance from Isaiah 61.2); I think it also covers form. There are some voices you have to listen to because they confront you with a remarkable personality. You listen to these people because of what they say. This is the key to Jesus's arresting preaching.

2. Bible preaching

And now this. Jesus created the effect he did in the Nazareth synagogue when he preached *from the Bible*. I wish I could make the Bible *come true* like that. I wish all our preachers could do it! And so, I guess, do most congregations, though not all, as I shall say in a minute. But how did Jesus use the Bible so as to make people listen? The key is in his opening words 'Today . . . this text has come true'. Jesus used the Bible in order to hear, and to cause others to hear, what God is saying *now*.

This is not easy. We must not fool ourselves. People, even good people, have read all manner of wrong-headed notions of their own into the scriptures. They have read Genesis 1 as if it were science and Revelation 17 as if it outlawed the Pope. We need scholarship to help us read the Bible properly, but when we read it we must not only hear the voice of Wellhausen, Bultmann or Käseman – or whoever is in the ascendant at the moment in the field of biblical studies – we must not only hear what Father X has to say about the passage or the latest sound Evangelical publication, we must hear what *the Lord God* is saying through the Scriptures today. This is how Jesus heard the Scriptures. This is how he used them in his preaching. This is why the people listened and all the mustiness was purged from those musty scrolls.

Sometimes this contemporary word of God is comforting, sometimes it stings. It stung terribly in the Nazareth synagogue when Jesus preached, so terribly that the congregation rushed him out of the place and up to the brow of the hill to finish him off. No more sermons like that please! The Bible can be boring, dry and deadly but when it *becomes* the word of God (note the word becomes) it can be disturbing. Who wants to hear it then? Who, for instance, wants to hear Jesus teaching on divorce now?

3. The real presence of God

Come back to the Nazareth synagogue that Sabbath day. See Jesus sitting there in the pulpit, the congregation all eyes and ears in expectancy. 'He began to speak: "Today", he said "in your very hearing this text has come true."' How had it come true? The plain answer is because the possibility of liberation from all that bound the people sitting in front of him at that moment was actually present in the real presence of Jesus, the liberator among them.

I don't know that there is anything more important in the ministry in public worship, perhaps in the Christian ministry altogether, than to help the presence of God to become real among us. I see this as the function of preaching in worship. I see it as the function of the Eucharist – to make us conscious of the real presence of God. Far too often we are conscious of the minister, or of one another (which is why we must not make too much of the Peace in the new eucharistic rites), or we are chiefly conscious of the particular form of worship being used. Far better that we should say with Jacob in Genesis 28 'How fearsome is this place. This is none other than the house of God, this is the gate of heaven.'

But I ask myself – Did I enter this church this morning with the thought that I was actually coming into the presence of God? Did you? Did I listen to the scripture passages read with any words at all in my mind, if not on my lips, such as 'What is God saying to me today by means of them?' Did you?

Let me tell you something that took place not long ago. There was appointed to a parish a new vicar; not a brilliant man, but a thoroughly good man and a devoted pastor. As it happened, someone was making a purchase at a business in the locality and was attended to by a member of that congregation. As a friendly gesture the question was voiced on leaving 'How do you like your new vicar?' 'Oh, he's all right' came the reply somewhat diffidently; and then this, *sotto voce*, as if it ought not to be said 'The trouble is, he's a bit too religious'.

Are there congregations, do you think, where worship which makes God real is *un*welcome? – it is too disturbing and people do not like to be disturbed. My guess is that this was the trouble at Nazareth when Jesus preached from the Bible. Men and women were suddenly confronted with the reality of God and themselves in his presence, and they did not like it. It happened because of the way Jesus preached from the Scriptures. 'Today, in your very hearing this text has come true.'

4. *Application*

And you say, 'What a tough word you have spoken today! Does not the presence of God cheer us, strengthen us and soothe us?' Yes, indeed, but not till we are shaken out of our complacency, our ruts and the casualness we so easily slide into with regard to our worship. Advent – and this is the second Sunday in Advent – is meant to shake us out of all this, for only when we have experienced Christ's disturbance can we experience his peace which he longs to give us. This is the gospel of Christ.

8. Light for all the World

Matthew 5.15 (NEB) '*When a lamp is lit, it is not put under the meal-tub, but on the lamp-stand, where it gives light to everyone in the house.*'

I wonder if Jesus possessed a sense of humour? I wonder if he was quick to see the comic side of things? Is this a stupid question? or a question that ought not to be asked? But was he not sensitive to incongruities? And do not incongruities make for comedy? What about his word picture of a blind man trying to lead another blind man! And a camel, hump and all, attempting to struggle through the eye of a needle! You don't know whether to laugh or cry. Is not this how we should hear Jesus's words from the so-called sermon on the mount 'When a lamp is lit, it is not put under the meal-tub'? Just as if anyone would!

But wait a minute. Suppose, just suppose, a father returning home from work after dark – and remember home in Jesus's day meant a one-roomed house only, where the entire family lived, ate and slept – suppose on opening the door he found the whole place in darkness. 'Hey, what has happened? Why hasn't someone lit the lamp?' Then a voice out of the darkness. 'We have, Dad, we have lit the lamp'. And then he lifts the meal-tub. There is the lamp duly lit and burning brightly when the tub is lifted. Would I be wrong to suggest that the perpetrator was Jesus himself as a little boy, just for a lark; and he remembered it?

Every single person in the church possesses a lit lamp or you would not be here as a worshipper. Your lit lamp is your faith in God. I cannot tell you how your lamp came to be lit because I do not know you personally, but lit it is, even if the flame is smoky. This however I can tell you, you did not light it yourself. Somehow it came to be lit. Somehow it *caught* light. Your faith, that is to say, was kindled by contact with someone else's faith; or by some words you heard or read, or some striking life of sacrificial service that appealed to you. Faith comes to be for reasons we cannot always trace or explain. This is why we call it a gift, something we did not make or earn ourselves. But this is the point Jesus made about the lamp. When it is lit 'it is not put under the meal-tub, but on the lamp-stand, where it gives light to everyone in the house'.

1. The ordained ministry

A few months ago I drew attention to these words of Jesus when preaching the sermon at the ordination of one man to the priesthood in the Anglican Pro-Cathedral in Brussels. I had taken some small part in this man's training and I knew him to be a man of personal faith in Christ as Lord, a faith which had been deepened, broadened and tested in his three years of theological training. It was an impressive service with a large congregation. I told the people that what we were doing in ordaining him to the priesthood was setting him and his faith up on a lamp-stand in the community. From henceforth people would see him as a man openly professing a distinctive faith, and not only that but a man who felt himself called to commend that faith wherever he was able. Especially would he be recognized as one authorized to celebrate the sacred elements of the faith, the mystical body and blood of Christ in the Eucharist. From the time of his ordination there would be no question of his hiding his light under a meal-tub or anything else. The ordination was public. The subsequent ministry would be public. When Jesus said a lamp is not put under a meal-tub he also said 'a town that stands on a hill *cannot* be hid'.

Perhaps it is singularly fitting that the words should be applied first of all to the ordained ministry of the Church. As St Matthew has recorded them they were addressed first of all to the inner circle of Jesus's disciples, though to the ears also of the multitude standing around on the mountain. No doubt those disciples were apprehensive as they thought of themselves as lamps on a lamp-stand for the whole community, unable to be hidden. This nevertheless was their calling and in due course they found themselves fulfilling it.

2. The ministry of the laity

It is a mistake however to reckon that the apostles as light-bearing lamp-stands existed as substitutes for the great body of Christian disciples. They were not appointed to function *instead* of the laity but rather to encourage and enable the laity *also* to function as light-bearing lamp-stands. So the ordained ministry in the Church today is meant to be an enabling ministry. Its responsibility and its privilege is so to burn brightly and to illuminate its surroundings that other lights become kindled by it. We might call them 'laity lights' – able to shine in dark places where the ordained ministry, separated as it is to a special ministry, cannot operate.

I have sometimes wondered if the relationship between the ordained ministry and the lay ministry in the total witness of the Church can be compared to that between the lighthouses around our coasts and the thousands of illuminated buoys that mark out the safe channels for shipping. There are seven hundred and fifty-four lighthouses around European coasts, some of them famous like Eddystone lighthouse and the striking red and white lighthouse off Beachy Head. Two of the wonders of the world were light-houses, the Pharos of Alexandria and the Colossus of Rhodes, but the great era of lighthouses began less than three hundred years ago, since when navigation at sea without them is unthinkable. But lighthouses alone are quite inadequate. Could you imagine a ship making its way down the winding estuary at Harwich for example out into the open North Sea without the marker buoys with their flashing lights indicating the safe channel? And when we are reminded that there are some twenty-thousand submerged wrecks in the North-Western sea approaches to Europe alone we get some idea of the importance of these lesser lights. I hesitate to liken those of us who are in the ordained ministry to our lighthouses with their powerful beams able to sweep the surrounding seas at night for twenty-five miles, though a list could be drawn up of Christian leaders who have acted like this as beacons of light in a dark world. I have however no hesitation in likening the rank and file of sincerity and faithful lay Christians to marker buoys at sea upon whose witness safe passage across the sea of life becomes possible.

Christian teachers, we need you. Christian trade unionists, we need you. And Christian married couples who keep their marriages and their homes intact. And Christian business men who do not cheat. And Christian employers who respect the persons of their employees. And Christian employees who do not steal from their employers. No, the light on the marker-buoy does not send a powerful beam of light across the darkened waters that surround it, but *it can be seen* and that is its function. Do not tell me you are only a housewife, only a fitter, only a secretary, only an insurance clerk. Your light where you are is what counts. Do not hide it. Jesus said, 'Where a lamp is lit, it is not put under the meal-tub, but on the lamp-stand, where it gives light to everyone in the house.' He also said 'Let your light so shine before men, that they may see your good works, and glorify your Father who is in heaven.'

3. *Reflected light*

At this point in our thinking both the ordained and the lay Christians need to be careful. Every man, woman and child has a unique light. Its existence is part of the glorious endowment of the human as human; one of its manifestations is the conscience. It is not to be despised, not to be trampled or trifled with, otherwise the ensuing darkness is darkness indeed. But there is a light outside us much more powerful. The fourth gospel clearly identifies it when it reports Jesus as saying, 'I am the light of the world. No follower of mine shall wander in the dark; he shall have the light of life.' When the Christian is up on his lamp-stand, it is not merely the light of the workings of his own conscience that he is allowing all to see, but the light of Christ which has kindled a new light within him. We might call it reflected light, the reflected light of Christ.

Come back to that sermon on the mount. As set out in St Matthew's gospel (chapter 5), immediately before Jesus said to his disciples 'When a lamp is lit, it is not put under the meal-tub', he prefaced it by this, 'You are the light of the world'. Imagine it! Put yourselves in those disciples' shoes! They were ordinary working men for the most part, some fishermen. 'You are the light of the world'! How ridiculous it must have sounded in their ears. And it was ridiculous, unless the all-important factor be taken into account that they were called to witness to Christ who is undoubtedly the light of the world.

Think if you can of what the story of our world would have been had there been no Christ in it. No, we cannot think of it. It is unthinkable. But with Christ there is light. There is the light of life. Light, that is, which makes life worthy of the name possible. This is what Christians reflect, and whenever they reflect it dark places, no matter in what part of the globe, are beginning to be illuminated.

'When a lamp is lit, it is not put under the meal-tub, but on the lamp-stand, where it gives light to everyone in the house.' That last phrase should not be missed – 'Light to everyone in the house'. You do not know, any one of you listening to me, what light you are giving to someone else by which he or she is finding a way in the circumstances that beset each of them. There is no reason why you should know. But God knows. He knows why he has kindled your light of life. All you need worry about, and I mean worry about, is to see that we do not hide that lamp under the meal-tub, or anything else. God will take care of the issues.

9. Discipline and Compassion

Matthew 5.17, 18 (NEB) *Do not suppose that I have come to abolish the Law and the prophets; I did not come to abolish, but to complete.*

I wonder what made Jesus say that. I wonder why he felt it necessary to defend his ministry. Was he aware of misunderstanding? Was he conscious that he might appear as if he were abolishing the Law and the prophets? As regards the Law, did he not heal on the sabbath day? And as for the prophets, if you omit the occasions when he 'tore strips off' the Pharisees (though I believe they were laments rather than attacks) he did not speak like an Old Testament eighth-century prophet, he did not inveigh against social unrighteousness such as 'joining house to house till there is no room', or going after strong drink till it inflames. No wonder that even as a prophet there was doubt how to categorize him. So, did Jesus come to abolish the Law and the prophets? Dogmatically he denied the charge. 'Do not suppose that I have come to abolish the Law and the prophets; I did not come to abolish but to complete.'

1. Discipline

Now we know. Jesus is not opposed to law and order. Jesus is no anarchist. Neither does liberty for him mean licence. Indeed his aim is to make the maintenance of law and order *more possible*

The Law to which Jesus referred is written with a capital L. The technical word for it is Torah. Basically it stands for the great *corpus* of ritual and ethical instructions contained in the Pentateuch which came to regulate the whole life of Israel and of the individual Jew; and to some extent still does. It was believed to represent the mind of God for his people. It helped to maintain them as the chosen people. It made them distinctive among the nations. It even operated as their way of salvation. And Jesus grew up with the Torah. He was a Jew. He died faithful to the Torah, he lived with it willingly all his days.

We who are non-Jews do not stand in this relationship to the Torah, but we cannot count ourselves in the following of Jesus if we sit lightly to law, if we despise discipline, if we fall into unregulated living. It is true, law is not our way of salvation. Our way is faith in Christ crucified and risen, but discipline is the guardian of our salvation. In default of discipline we are in danger of losing what we have. Appetites must therefore be controlled – food, drink, drugs, sex, gambling and pugnaciousness. The Christian life must never be like a disorderly house. No good will come from a disorderly life.

And not only is discipline the way of safety, it is the way of achievement. Do you think Torvill and Dean, the champion ice dancers, would ever have reached world fame apart from an iron discipline? And why all this fuss on the part of an army commander to have his troops smart with polished boots and buttons? It is the disciplined force that wins battles. It is the organized man who reaches the top. Reading the life of Field Marshal Lord Alanbrooke, Chief of the Imperial General Staff during the last war and largely responsible for its conduct, I was fascinated to note how he wasted no opportunity to master situations. Not content with fluency in French and German, when he found himself in India he learned two Indian languages, and when in Egypt he immediately sent for a teacher of Arabic. Excellence is impossible without discipline, mastery impossible without application. No one who achieves anything drifts.

For all his emphasis on compassion, freedom and forgiveness, Jesus, let it be repeated, did not come to abolish law, he came to complete it. Christians saved by grace cannot sit lightly to law. The ten commandments are still necessary. Jesus did not abrogate them.

2. Compassion

Law however – and this is my second point – can be harsh.

Successful people can be harsh. Financial profit as the only criterion of an enterprise can even be cruel. And far too often those who can master themselves despise those who hump along at the bottom of society with never a chance to make any kind of grade at all. The misfits, the incompetent and the incapacitated, the clumsy, the dimwitted. It is one of the distinguishing marks of the Hebrew prophets that they cared about the poor and downtrodden, and roundly condemned the successful who prided themselves on how faithfully they observed the minutiae of the ritual law.

Jesus added his weight to the keeping of the Law and the necessity for discipline. Yes, but in the same way as he did not come to abolish the Law so he did not come to destroy the prophets. On the contrary his ministry was conspicuous for the compassion he showed for sinners and the outcasts for whom no one cared, going out of his way to meet their needs. To give them a chance was the motive behind his action as it was behind that of the Hebrew prophets pleading for *social* righteousness. Jesus did not abolish their prophetic concern for the community, he completed it.

3. Inspiration

And now the conclusion stares us in the face. If we are to be faithful followers of Christ we must adhere to the necessity for law and order but we must not stop there. We must allow ourselves to be inspired with compassion for the underdogs in our world. This is the balance that needs to be kept, a balance in the individual life and a balance for which the Christian must strive in the community. Indeed there is here some indication of what a community entitled to call itself Christian must be – an orderly community and a compassionate community. Being an orderly community it will probably be successful, and being compassionate it will be saved from the destructiveness that issues from rebellious dissatisfaction.

I do not believe this wholesome balance is easy of attainment. I doubt if political policy alone can foster it. This is so because man is a sinful creature, which means that self-centredness and self-interest have a way of coming out on top. But in the following of Christ this can be overcome and is often gloriously overcome. So Christians can be a guiding light in the community for its welfare. We need Christians in local government, central government and in industry. We need what they stand for to shape public opinion. Christ is the saviour of the community as well as of the individual. Jesus came for both of them.

10.   The Sociable Christ

Luke 7.36 (NEB)   *One of the Pharisees invited him (Jesus)*
to dinner.

1. Social occasions

I don't suppose the invitation was conveyed by means of a white
card –

Simon
Member of the Pharisaic Party
requests the pleasure of the company of
Jesus of Nazareth
to dinner

7.30 for 8   *Black tie*

Nevertheless, however it was conveyed, it was not unlike an invitation we might ourselves give or receive. The point to notice is
that Jesus accepted such invitations; and not only on one occasion.
Two others are recorded in St Luke's gospel, both from Pharisees.
Apparently Jesus frequently went out to dinner. The fourth gospel
tells us that he even *began* his ministry at a party.

(a) Cheerfulness

Apparently these social meals were anything but solemn occasions, indeed they were so much the reverse that the religious
leaders of the day (who reckoned they knew how one purporting to
be a religious leader should conduct himself and encourage his
followers to conduct themselves) complained bitterly. The absence
of asceticism and the general merriment in Jesus's company appal-
led them. They made their feelings plain. But what Jesus said in
defence is illuminating. Nothing about any kind of policy of
appearing cheerful as becomes those with a gospel; simply that it
was impossible to be gloomy so long as they were together. Which
of course speaks volumes about the kind of guest Jesus must have
been. He radiated happiness. And of the course the twelve men
whom people recognized as his disciples adored him. How could
they not?

(b) Wisdom

But the table fellowship was not endlessly lighthearted, and certainly not empty. The twelve had questions to ask, and Jesus had comments to make on current affairs. Then everyone sat still, and out would come one of those marvellous parables of his, so engaging, so easy (at least on the surface); but everyone was 'left standing' by the subtle penetration of its wisdom. And when the party broke up, no doubt they said one to another, 'Where does he get it all from?'

Cheerfulness and wisdom then – which reminds me of an experience I had as a curate many years ago. I had been invited to a lunch party at which William Temple, the Archbishop of York, was the chief guest. As a mere curate I was seated a long way down the table and looked with awe at those privileged to sit next to the great man and hear his wisdom. After all at that time it was commonly said that he possessed one of the six finest minds in Europe. But what came over to me at that party was the uproarious peels of laughter which burst forth every now and again from the Archbishop's end of the table, his laughter by far the loudest. When I mentioned this to one or two people afterwards they told me that that laugh was frowned upon by some as being most unbecoming for an archbishop. I have since wondered if he was not on that account in very good company indeed. The Pharisees made the same kind of complaint about Jesus of Nazareth.

2. A Pharisee's dinner party

We return to the occasion when 'one of the Pharisees invited him (Jesus) to dinner'. We know this Pharisee's name. It was Simon. Simon turned out to be a poor host. To begin with he blatantly omitted the politeness which should accompany the arrival of a guest. Probably he thought this unnecessary for a preacher 'of no fixed abode'. But Jesus observed the omission and remarked on it. He could be disconcertingly straight. Then a woman slipped in. This was possible in the open planning of an Eastern household. Clearly she knew Jesus. That settled it for Simon. He had invited him in order to get to know him (what are social occasions for?), but with the presumption that he was a charlatan. The appearance of the woman confirmed his suspicion. Jesus however was too quick for Simon. 'Do you see this woman?' He certainly saw her! And then, with all the other guests waiting (we can be certain) there tripped off Jesus's lips one of the shortest but one of the most subtle of all the parables recorded in the gospels, in which forgiveness was not only implied for the woman's unsavoury past but also the

Pharisee's respectable past. I can't think what happened next because the New Testament does not say. But this is perfectly plain – and this is my second major point. Jesus of Nazareth was charming as a guest, sought after for his cheerfulness and wisdom; *but* whoever thought to put Jesus where he wanted him would soon be smarting with the knowledge that the reverse process had taken place. Whoever attempts to condemn Jesus discovers at the end of the day that he has condemned himself.

3. The eucharistic meal

There is one other supper party to which reference must be made, the last one at which Jesus was present. And this time he was the host, not the guest. All twelve disciples received an invitation to be present, including Judas. It got off to a bad start because there was an unseemly scramble for the best seats, but under Jesus's influence it settled down.

(a) Buoyancy

As the meal progressed an unusual solemnity was sensed by every guest. Jesus began to speak of betrayal, and Judas left the table. Then he took bread, blessed it, broke it and gave it to all present. Likewise with a cup of wine. Then, doubtless looking around the assembled company, he said, 'Do this in remembrance of me'.

And so it has come about that the Christian Church provides a kind of meal table, the Holy Communion, at which Christ is the host, albeit unseen, and we are the invited guests. This then is the pressing question. What should be the nature of this table fellowship? Can there be any doubt if it is to be in the following of those meals Jesus attended, and *gave*, during his earthly life? It should be buoyant, cheerful and warm. Of every act of Christian worship, thanksgiving should be the outstanding characteristic.

(b) Awe

But there is something else. A sense of *awe* should also be conspicuous. Simon the Pharisee treated the table fellowship to which he invited Jesus casually. What Jesus said on that occasion put Simon in his place. There is justification for alleging that modern man needs to be put in his place with regard to Christ. Christ is popular at the moment. Not only did *Jesus Christ Superstar* have a long run on the West End stage but there are plenty of people claiming Jesus as brother in their philanthropic moods and enterprises. 'He is with us in our social compassion, our reforming zeal, and our concern for the underdog.' Some go as far as to claim Jesus as their inspirer in freedom fighting. This will not do. We cannot claim Christ for anything. On the contrary he claims us. He is our lord and master before he is our brother, which is why a sense of reverence and awe is proper in all our Christian worship. We cannot be 'chummy' with God.

(c) Teaching

Thirdly we should note that Jesus used these occasions of table fellowship for teaching. Schillebeeckx, the Dutch theologian, may be right when he suggests that the parables of Jesus were not delivered in his preaching to the crowds but when his disciples and others were gathered in social intercourse over a meal. The parables represent *Tischreden*, as the Germans call it, 'table talk'. St Luke chapter 14 certainly looks that way. There has been a certain impatience with teaching and preaching in the course of worship these last two or three decades. But our worship addressed to God will be incomplete unless there is also a word addressed to us *from* God; without it the *fellowship* will be one-sided, it will be incomplete.

The gospel needs not only to be celebrated, it needs to be spoken. And this is what it says. God will have us if we lay aside self-justification. God will have us in his fellowship not because we are good but because of what the Eucharist re-enacts and celebrates – the life, death and resurrection of Jesus. And when we accept that we are invited to his table and *accepted* we rise in stature as Christ's people, and our conduct shows it. We become Christians in action.

11. No Ruthless Uprooting

Matthew 13.30   *'Let both grow together until the harvest.'*

Some time ago a missionary told me that this text put her in an embarrassing position. She could almost have wished that Jesus had never told the parable where it occurs. It was like this. Her African gardener simply would not keep the garden weeded. And when she could stand the untidiness no longer she reproved him as strongly as she knew how. 'Well, Mam,' he replied confidently 'Did not de good Lord in de parable about de weeds in de field say "Let both grow together till the harvest?" That be just what I be doing, Mam, just that.'

My sermon, like the gospel for today, is about weeds. Most of us who have anything to do with gardens hate them. I see you can purchase a chemical which purports to eliminate weeding altogether! Do you believe it? But why do we have weeds at all? I guess the gardening experts will tell us they indicate fertility in the soil – but that doesn't help me. And I can think of an extension of the question much harder. Why do we have evil in the world? Why suffering? why pain? why crushing disappointment? why marriages that go wrong? It is the *volume* of suffering that baffles. Since the world began life has been for millions and millions of people little short of a slow death. I have often thought there must be enough tears in the world to rival the Pacific Ocean. And if all this seems light years away for us sitting in this lovely chapel (Chapel Royal, St James's Palace, London) this morning is there one of us who has never asked why when we have tried to do the right thing the outcome has been the exact opposite? What is this apparent 'cussedness' in life which seems to bedevil even our best attempts to build a better world? Always, always, there seems to be lurking in the shadows something, someone, bent on spoiling the *good* things we try to fashion. This is the heartrending question the gospel for today handles, 'Sir, didst not thou sow good seed in thy field? – whence then hath it tares?'

1. The origin of evil

I have been reading again the novels of Thomas Hardy. Was there ever an artist in words to compare with him in depicting human nature and the world of nature? But almost all his stories are tragic stories because he saw human beings as the playthings of capricious fate. This, as for the ancient Greeks, was his explanation of the weeds, the tares, in the field of life – *capricious fate*.

I expect Hardy, who was an unhappy man, was reacting against the Genesis story which says that evil enters life when people rebel against the sovereignty of God, reckoning that we can fare better without his dominion. I see the difficulty. I mean, how can you say the incidence of earthquakes, typhoons, and flooding on a vast scale as in India and China has anything to do with man's rebellion against God's sovereignty? So I can appreciate writers like Teilhard de Chardin who point out that the world is *evolving*, so our troubles are part of the growing process. Unfortunately, however, this tidy scientific explanation fails to take into account the devilish nature of man's inhumanity to man – torture, terrorism, kneecapping, child bashing, slave labour. And it is not decreasing – the sort of horror being perpetrated in many parts of the world today. So we need not be surprised if some seek an explanation in the existence of dark and evil *spiritual* forces at work, the sort of evil we used to think of as the devil before we became so sophisticated and laughed him out as a ridiculous figure in red tights and a forked tail. The blunt fact however is that words like 'diabolical' and 'devilish' will not go away.

What is the explanation for the existence of weeds, for the existence of evil in the world? 'Sir, didst not thou sow good seed in thy field, from whence then hath it tares?' Perhaps all three theories I have listed have something in them, all three that is except Hardy's. But isn't our real worry not any theory about the origin of evil but what to *do* about it, how to counteract it?

2. Dealing with evil

So we come back to Jesus's parable, our gospel for today, 'Sir, didst not thou sow good seed in thy field, from whence then hath it tares?' And he said 'An enemy hath done this'. Actually while men slept the enemy came and sowed tares among the wheat and went his way. So the servants faced their master with this urgent question – 'Wilt thou then that we go and gather them up?' Quick, ruthless action was what they were calling for as the way to tackle evil in the world. Root it out! It seemed reasonable enough and men have tried it, are still trying it. It was the way of Lenin, Stalin, Chairman Mao and Marxism generally. Never mind the means, it is the end that counts. So the killings, the deportation, the starvings, the forced labour camps. Ruthlessness is the way. Ruthless uprooting. 'Wilt thou then that we go and gather them up?' And the answer of the parable is, 'No'.

Why is this? Because those tares, or that darnel (which is the technical name for the plant here) when they begin to grow are almost indistinguishable from the wheat. So if you go in for ruthless uprooting you will be bound to ruin what you are most keen to preserve. The separation process is only safe at harvest time by winnowing or sifting. So the servants received a categorical refusal. 'No; lest while ye gather up the tares, ye root up also the wheat with them.'

Fair enough, you say, in the cornfield – but what about the field called the world? Do we let evil rip? Do we sit back and do nothing?

3. Three lessons

(a) There are I think three lessons here, and the first is for the *Church*. It must never involve itself in campaigns whose declared aim is the uprooting of specific ills in society. Recognize them, yes! Lift up its voice against them, yes! But ruthless uprooting, no! This is why the Church must be very careful how it becomes involved in any kind of political action in any part of the world. Does this surprise us? or even dismay us? But consider the life and work of Jesus. Were there not social abuses in plenty in his day? Oppression by a foreign power. The grinding of the poor. Crippling taxes. The use of human beings as slaves with no human rights at all. Yet he did not join, or even verbally ally himself with any of the liberation movements of his day; the Zealots, the Herodians, the Essenes. He did not support their policy of ruthless uprooting and nor should the Church, which professes to follow him.

(b) Secondly, a lesson for *Government*, whose responsibility it certainly is not only to recognize evil in the community but to deal with it. Law and order must prevail. But if it pursues a policy of ruthless suppression it will destroy more than it creates. It is an empirical fact that suppression does not lead to liberty, nor violence to peace. Taking the sword may be a necessary evil but an evil it remains and should never be resorted to unless there is no other way.

(c) Thirdly, today's parable tells us *something about God* – and I have a strong conviction that no sermon is a proper sermon unless it does tell us something about him. And what does it say? That God himself is not ruthless. Whatever evil there may be growing in the world, or for that matter in us, he will not pursue a course of ruthless action to uproot it. If he counsels against it for his servants he will not engage in it for himself.

I am inclined to think that this is not without immediate

relevance to the widespread contemporary fear about the total destruction of this earth through nuclear missiles. I am not so poor a theologian as not to know that God does not intervene to protect man from the consequences of his own free-will. Nevertheless, this is God's world. He has created it. He has sown good seed in his field and he does not want the whole crop jeopardized by man's ruthless and intemperate action. Most of the discussion about nuclear arms goes on without any reference to God whatsoever. If however we do allow today's gospel parable to speak its message to us about the nature of God, I for one am not without hope for the future.

My sermon today has been about weeds and how *not* to deal with them. I would rather, however, leave you thinking not about the weeds in the parable but about him who told the parable. He was a strong character and could be very disconcerting. But he never treated anyone roughly, not even notorious sinners, much less the 'weedy' people in his society. All of which encourages me to believe that when my time comes to meet him face to face, tenderness and patience, and not ruthlessness, will be the order of the final judgment day. It is a gospel I count it a privilege to proclaim. It is the good news of Jesus Christ.

12. Popular Religion

John 6.26 (RV) *'Ye seek me, not because ye saw the signs but because ye ate of the loaves and were filled.'*

It was a sunny afternoon in November, warm and calm, when our party of about a dozen reached Capernaum's minute quayside situated on the North Western shore of the lake of Galilee. We visited the ruins of the synagogue and tried to imagine what it must have been like. There was scarcely anyone about and so peaceful was this Saturday afternoon that it was difficult to conceive that it had ever been crowded or that anything significant had ever taken place there. But it had. Jesus said some hard things in that synagogue which constituted a turning point in the public's attitude towards him. The crisis point was reached when a crowd of five thousand and more (that is a capacity audience for the Albert Hall in London) raced round the head of the lake, and from many other directions, wild with enthusiasm bent on crowning him king of

Galilee. The ruling authorities would have seen it as a *coup d'état* in the making and crushed it immediately.

1. The popularity of Jesus

There were two reasons for this surge of popularity, one cumulative, the other immediate. The first was the healings Jesus performed. We need not be surprised. Anyone who has resigned himself to the presence of incurable suffering and then seen it lifted is seized with an elation clamouring for an outlet. Jesus had performed many such cures. No wonder the excitement over him was electric. And there was also the immediate cause. Five thousand men, besides women and children, had been fed from five barley loaves and two small fishes.

I cannot explain this feeding and do not intend to try. The Dutch Roman Catholic theologian Schillebeeckx points out how two opposite and extreme views about the miracles of Jesus are both wrong. One is to assert that since the miracles evidently broke through natural law they prove Jesus to be divine. The other is the *a priori* dictum that natural law cannot under any circumstances be set aside and, therefore, the miracles did not take place. But there is a more penetrating question. Of what stature must Jesus have been and of what order did his actions partake to cause a reaction so powerful that one set of people responded with the assertion – he is in league with the devil, and the other set – he is divine?

In the light of this polarization I cannot go along with those preachers who satisfy themselves that they have explained the feeding of the five thousand when they have asserted that Jesus persuaded the boy with the picnic basket of five barley loaves and two small fishes to share it with those who had none. Others copied him. So all were fed. This was the miracle! Leave aside the consequent awkward question as to how in that case there were 'twelve filled basketfuls of scraps' (Mark 6.43) picked up afterwards, and concentrate on the basic point – something stupendous must have taken place to set alight the existing popular enthusiasm for Jesus, so burning that the crowds gathered to force kingship on Jesus. No one contemplated this because of a shared picnic!

2. The popularity tested

Now what strikes me about this miracle is that strictly speaking it was unnecessary, that is on the grounds of human physical need. The crowds had not been caught in some sudden harsh predicament. They were not a famine-stricken people. Hunger was not eating away their humanity (it can do this). No floods had ruined their crops or swept away their houses. No disaster of any kind such as Bangladesh and the Yangtse valley have suffered. It was not even winter but the full tide of spring with fields covered with fresh green grass. Some inconvenience no doubt, and some discomfort, but on those grounds divine intervention can scarcely be justified. Indeed the disciples' suggestion that the crowds should disperse to the local farms and villages to purchase food was not unreasonable; and if those who carried some emergency rations could be persuaded to share what they had this might provide a temporary sufficiency which after all was all that was required.

So why the miracle? This is the question the fourth Gospel handles since the other three have not faced it. Is it not the case that the miracle was not wrought in the first place to feel the hungry? Though in fact it did so. Nor was it carried out in order to provide a practical lesson about caring for the starving masses, though it has done this and rightly so. No, this miracle was performed as a tactical action on the part of Jesus who, like a general, knew what he would do. This the fourth gospel makes plain (6.6). It was carried out in order to bring the dangerous misplaced popular enthusiasm for him to a head and *explode* it. The action was dangerous. The explosion was dangerous. Jesus gave the crowds the slip. Crowds bent on collective action do not take kindly to being given the slip. An ugly situation developed, so ugly for safety's sake Jesus pressed his disciples to push off in their boat across the lake while he took to the hills.

Darkness fell. Next morning the crowds were still there on the shore disgruntled, angry and puzzled, knowing that the one boat had conveyed only the disciples away. Where was Jesus? To find out they made for the other side of the lake and came across him at Capernaum. 'Rabbi, when did you come here?' they asked. And this was his reply (today's text) 'Ye seek me, not because ye saw the signs but because ye ate of loaves and were filled'. It was a 'brush off'. Later in the synagogue he set out at length what his mission was. Those who heard him found his words hard. His mission was to provide spiritual food, in fact the bread of life. They did not like it. They began to feel they had 'got him wrong'. And when this feeling worked its way in, then their resentment festered angrily. They would wash their hands of him. Worse, they would be rid of him. Religion is all right providing it is useful. It is endurable, even popular so long as it cures the incurable and feeds the hungry; but not otherwise, there are better things to do. What happens then if that enthusiasm *for* degenerates into enthusiasm *against*. It happened at Capernaum after the feeding of the five thousand. From there the road to Christ's cross began to be laid down.

3. Popular religion tested

Perhaps we do not readily see ourselves in this picture, but is it all that uncommon for religion to be valued primarily for its material benefits? Religion is a safeguard against Communism – and to some extent it is. Religion in the home and in the schools would do much to prevent vandalism – and there is truth in this. Religion by reason of the integrity and honesty it inculcates makes for prosperity – so it does. If even a significant check was applied to the current petty pilferings, stealing, cheating and downright robbery that goes on in Britain today, putting up the costs of industry by thousands of millions annually, the whole population would be better off forthwith. Religion is good for the community. There is of course such a phenomenon as bad religion, bad for the community, there have been wars of religion. Nevertheless the general truth stands, religion holds society together. Politicians of the first rank know this. Here, however, is a deeper truth which the incident of the feeding of the five thousand and its sequel drives home. If we seek religion *because it is useful*, if we want Christ *because* he can be profitable, if what we have our eye set upon are the material and physical benefits, even comforts, that in the long run accrue thereby for the community, we shall not find our way to God and the life eternal, we may even discover only bad religion, a dangerous commodity.

Here is the test. A religion which has no practice of worship in it, no spontaneous worship, a religion which does not seek as its primary aim communion with God, a religion which will not be adhered to if it involves on occasion sacrifice and even ridicule, such a religion we may be sure is only really concerned with religion's possible *benefits*. It is sought because it is useful. And then the words of Jesus at Capernaum apply. 'Ye seek me not because ye saw the signs' (that is, the signs of *God's* presence) 'but because ye ate of the loaves and were filled.' From that kind of religion Christ separates himself.

There is one other lesson from this story. Jesus of Nazareth suspected the shoddy basis of the popular enthusiasm for himself and decided to put it to the test. So often we think of God testing our faith by means of hardship, illness or maybe some hurting 'let down'. Similarly with recruits being sifted in the army for commandos. Severe training is the test. I read the other day that when Prince Edward joined the Royal Marines under the University Cadet Entrance Scheme his training officer said 'His feet won't touch the ground. He won't know what hit him.' No doubt God tests and trains us similarly by the experiences of life. Sometimes, however, the test comes in the form of prosperity, a good job, a remarkable recovery from illness. So Jesus tested the crowds of Galilee. Not with a famine to see if they would stay faithful in adversity, but with prosperity, with five thousand miraculously fed. They failed. They failed miserably. Their superficiality stood out a mile. They only wanted Christ because they thought he would be useful for the economy. So they drifted away. We ought not to forget this lesson. An indication of the genuineness of our religion is whether or not we hold on to it when things are going well.

13. Transfiguration

Mark 9.2 (NEB)   *Six days later Jesus took Peter, James, and John with him and led them up a high mountain where they were alone; and in their presence he was transfigured.*

I wonder if you have ever felt horribly alone? No, I do not mean as a stranger in some foreign capital where everyone speaks in a language you do not understand. Nor do I mean the experience of tramping across some desolate moorland and before you have reached your destination darkness has all but closed in and there is no sound but your own soft footfalls, and maybe a screech of some startled bird. I mean the experience of having something on your mind about which you cannot talk even to your closest friends. They just would not understand. It could be an interview you have to face in a few days' time, the thought of which keeps you awake at nights. It could be the knowledge that with the rising cost of living you see no way of keeping the house and home going as it has been and sooner or later you will have to tell the family. It could be some secret about you which will be public knowledge before long, and how will you face the tittle-tattle? There is such a thing as being alone in a crowd, horribly alone, alone with the longing to tell someone – but it is impossible. No one would understand. You are horribly alone.

1. The time of the transfiguration

I do not think we shall begin to appreciate what the synoptic gospels tell us about the transfiguration of Jesus unless we see how it took place when he was horribly alone with no one to whom he could talk. I doubt if we shall wholly appreciate it *even then* because it touches on such mysteries as psychic phenomena and the state of being when these mortal bodies of ours have passed away. All this I shall have to leave on one side. What I suggest is something simpler. I suggest Jesus of Nazareth will mean more to us in his humanity and seem closer if we begin at the point of his horrible aloneness at the stage of his ministry when the transfiguration occurred. There was something on his mind, something terrible which not even his closest disciples could begin to understand, so wrapped up were they in their own ideas.

What was this something? It was his own crucifixion he knew could not be far off. I have often wondered if Jesus had seen a crucifixion. Crucifixions were not uncommon. The Romans used them as a deterrent for slaves against rebellion. Jesus would certainly know about them. No doubt he had witnessed the brutality of which the Roman occupying army was capable in keeping down Judaea. How did he sleep with such a prospect before him? And how horrible his aloneness in knowing that his disciples, not even Peter, possessed the wit to see the course events were bound to take, given the conflict that had broken out between Jesus and the religious authorities of his day on account of his teaching. The disciples to a man had no thought but that they were marching to Zion, beautiful, beautiful Zion, where there would stand a throne for Jesus and his faithful followers. The land would welcome him as king – Hosanna to the Son of David! Long live the King! How could Jesus talk to men with notions as naïve as this? How could he tell them that a cross not a crown awaited him at the end of the road. They simply would not understand. He was horribly alone.

We once had an Archbishop of Canterbury who lived with such a nightmare as this. He was Thomas Cranmer. Charged with the heresy of Protestantism his accusers imprisoned him in Oxford where attempts were made to cause him to recant. He knew of course that if he did not he would be burned at the stake. And aware of the fact that he had not been present at any burning himself on 16 October 1555 he was stood on the roof of the prison and made to watch his two friends Ridley and Latimer led out to the town ditch just beyond the northern walls to suffer this fate. It was horrible. Latimer was quickly suffocated by the smoke but Ridley's pile burned slowly and when his brother-in-law tried to shorten the agony by adding more fuel it only succeeded in slowing down the fire. Ridley was still alive and screaming after his legs had been burned away. It was not till 21 March 1556 that Cranmer was sent to the stake. He knew what was coming. He had seen that burning six months before. How did he sleep with this on his mind? Let me say this. We shall not grasp the context of the event in Jesus's life called the transfiguration unless we see it in this kind of context. Jesus was in an agony of mind. He was almost at breaking point and horribly alone.

2. The purpose of the transfiguration

Then the transfiguration came. It came to reassure Jesus. It came to give him strength to go on, courage to take that terrible road to Jerusalem at the end of which stood a gibbet waiting. All this it accomplished by drawing back for a moment the veil hiding the glory which lies on the other side of the pain and suffering of this world but which assuredly is there. Also by letting this lonely pilgrim see how the faithful who have gone on before watch with understanding and approbation, as if in a grandstand, how he will 'run the race that is set before him'. And thirdly, it stiffened his resolve by voicing in recognizable words – had he not heard them before at the beginning of his ministry? – the care and closeness of God himself who had chosen him to accomplish at Jerusalem what no one else before or since has ever managed.

But what was this transfiguration? What does the word mean? It means a temporary alteration of the outward appearance. The person looks different. The story which all three synoptic gospels record tells of Jesus climbing a high mountain (was it Hermon?) with three specially selected disciples, Peter, James and John. They saw nothing different in him as they toiled up those steep slopes hour after hour, but at the lonely summit when he began to pray they scarcely recognized him. There was a translucence about his being far beyond what any glistening white garments could possibly accomplish. He was in another world, beyond the world of space and time; and so were they to witness it. No, I cannot explain this. I can lay claim to no psychic gifts, but those with extrasensory perception do not find this whole incident utterly beyond them. Some claim to see every single person with a distinctive aura around them. It was the feeling after this that made extra-holy men be depicted by paintings with haloes round their heads. Let those who can receive this receive it. I can do no more than note how Moses and Elijah appeared in this vision talking with the transfigured Jesus. They were talking about this death he was about to accomplish at Jerusalem, actually calling it (according to St Luke) an exodus. Both these great leaders from the past, according to the tradition, had been spared a horrible martyrdom. Why then crucifixion for Jesus? And why compare it to Moses leading his people out of the slavery of Egypt? Peter, one of the three onlookers, understood none of this. All he asked for was permanent residence forthwith in this scene of heavenly existence without the pain of death; but he did not know what he was talking about. So the spell was broken but not without a voice from heaven calling 'This is my Son, my chosen, listen to him'. Immediately they were back in the world of space and time and Jesus was seen to be alone. He did not speak to the three about what had taken place. How could he? they did not understand, but he was not so horribly alone as he had been. Reassurance had been granted him about what lay ahead. It was not some awful mistake. It would not be wasted effort. He would find the courage to go through with it. This was what the transfiguration meant to Jesus, at least this.

3. A meaning for us

What can it mean for us? Very little perhaps. If so we had better avoid the error of Peter on the holy mount and not speak when we do not understand. And if we have to be content with a common verdict of contemporary literary criticism that here we have a post-resurrection story of Jesus, written back into the pre-crucifixion and resurrection period for theological purposes, so be it. But has it nothing to say to ordinary men and women today? Does it not bring Jesus of Nazareth close to the experience of almost every one of us? Who is there who knows nothing of apprehension about the future? Who is there by the time of drawing his or her old age pension that gives not even a passing thought to what our end will be, and when, and where? Of course we cannot talk about it, which is why at times there is the feeling of being horribly alone. Is it not possible then to hear in this transfiguration story some word of God addressed to us, not least that Christ understands our loneliness, he experienced it himself? And can we not look for reassurance that in the end all will be well even if there are pains to be endured? And can we not, knowing all will be well, find a courage which without this reassurance might utterly fail? I believe we can, because even if we lack all mystical gifts of psychic insight we have the evidence of Christ's own resurrection that all will be well, a resurrection which has proved itself exceedingly hard to explain away.

But transfiguration? Are we to be transfigured? Beyond the grave I believe we are. We shall be the same but we shall be different. But transfigured now in this life? Is this possible? Does this make sense? Yet, who is there who has not seen someone transfigured? Thackeray in his novel *Pendennis* tells of a girl called Laura whom he, Pendennis, left behind as a lumping schoolgirl almost unrecognizable when he returned after two years, she had grown so beautiful. And if we classify this as physical and natural, what of the young woman whom the prospect of marriage makes radiant? This is mental, even spiritual transfiguration; we speak of a new light in the eye, even of a light of life. But there is something more profound to which the transfiguration of Jesus when he was praying points us. It is the change that comes over a man or woman who has heard the voice of God calling to them individually, 'You are my son, you are my daughter'. It is the relationship to God which is personalized in the sacrament of the Eucharist – 'The body of Christ, the blood of Christ keep *you* in eternal life'. Perhaps it is too much to expect that the communicant will leave the altar rail with a shining face like those coming down from the mount of God's real presence, but the awareness of God's care for us for time and eternity certainly does transform our outlook on life. We are the same people and yet we are different people. Transfigured as Christ was on the mountain top? No, this is not possible for us. But transfigured by our faith in the Christ transfigured, crucified and risen for us? Yes, that is perfectly possible. I have seen evidence that it has taken place.

14.   A First Sight of the Cross

Mark 10.52 (NEB)   '*And at once he recovered his sight and followed him on the road.*'

On Friday morning 28 May 1982 I turned on the television at 8.45 in order to see the Pope arrive at Gatwick. I was just in time to hear David Dimbleby say 'The Pope's plane is now about eight miles from Gatwick and is passing over Lingfield'. I looked out of the window (our house in Lingfield faces south) and there it was! A beautiful sight! I could scarcely believe it. The Pope was passing over our village. I am not sure if I waved, but if I didn't I ought to have done.

1. Jesus's approach to Jerusalem

I cannot suggest that when Jesus approached Jerusalem, passing through the city of Jericho, the expectation and build-up could possibly compare with the publicity that accompanied Pope John's visit to Britain; but *it was that kind of occasion* as St Mark has portrayed it. Three times over in the compass of twenty-two verses he emphasizes Jerusalem as the destination of Jesus's journey. 'They were on the road, going up to Jerusalem, Jesus leading the way' (10.32); 'He took the Twelve aside and began to tell them what was to happen to him. "We are now going to Jerusalem" he said' (10.33); 'They were now approaching Jerusalem' (11.1).

He was not making the journey alone, nor even solely with the twelve disciples. A great crowd of pilgrims accompanied him making it almost a triumphal procession, all bent on attending the great festival in the capital city. In the crowd there would be chanting, praying and merrymaking as well. And with each stage of the journey expectation would be heightened till parents could announce to their children 'Tomorrow you will see it with your own eyes – the city of Zion – and it will take your breath away!' And this time there was an added excitement. Jesus the prophet of Nazareth in Galilee was in that crowd of pilgrims. What then might happen when he of all people reached Jerusalem? They could scarcely wait. Perhaps history would at last turn in favour of the Jewish people.

2. A blind man

So they came to Jericho, the last stopping place before the ascent to Jerusalem. And then it happened. Such a trifling incident in its way, but no one forgot it. It came to be written into the history of Jericho, and heaven knows the city was packed tight enough with startling history. But all three synoptic gospels record it. A blind man begging by the roadside making himself a nuisance by shouting out to Jesus as he passed by, such a nuisance that the people rounded on him, trying to shut him up. No one wanted the spell of this messianic procession up to Jerusalem (if that is what it was) broken by some insensitive gutter squatter. But Jesus caught the title by which the blind beggar was addressing him. It was a messianic title. 'Son of David, Jesus, have pity on me.' And the more the crowds attempted to silence him the louder did he shout his *Kyrie eleison*.

Then Jesus stopped. (Surely this must be an eyewitness account. Something like this did actually happen in Jericho.) People never forgot it. They remembered details. Jesus stopped still in the roadway. I guess the whole procession stopped. Of course it did. Silence fell so that the shouting sounded even more sonorous. 'Son of David, Jesus, have pity on me.' 'Call him', commanded Jesus, speaking like the king he was. Someone did just that, adding 'Take heart; stand up; he is calling you'. The blind man needed no further bidding. He threw aside his cloak (another possible indication that here we have an eyewitness account). Was the cloak spread out before him as a receptacle for coins? Anyway he left all behind. 'He sprang up and came to Jesus.' So with the crowd as spectators these two men faced each other – the beggar with no light in his eye at all and he whom we have come to call 'the light of the world'. Then the question from Jesus's lips 'What do you want me to do for you?' Little can be done for the man who does not know what he wants. This one however knew, 'Master, I want my sight back'. No anointing followed nor laying on of hands, only the words 'Go; your faith has cured you.' St Mark says, 'And at once he recovered his sight'. But the cure is not quite all. Indeed we miss the clue to the significance of this incident if we overlook the closing words, '(he) followed him on the road'.

3. What the once blind man saw

Some commentators on this scripture tell us that this following of

Jesus by the erstwhile blind beggar is not to be taken literally. It means 'became a disciple', like Simon of Cyrene for instance. I do not doubt it, but the three words 'on the road' tacked on at the end suggest to me that they should be read in conjunction with 10.32 'They were *on the road*, going up to Jerusalem, Jesus leading the way'. This cured man now, with seeing eyes, actually joined the procession. So I ask myself, 'Was his breath taken away' when he saw Jerusalem for the first time as they climbed the steep ascent from Jericho? Did he bivouac with the other pilgrims for the whole Festival week close to the city? Did he watch Jesus ride in triumph on a donkey into the temple area? Did he hear how Jesus had been arrested, tried, flogged and led out to be crucified? Was he there with the crowds watching the slow, obscene torture of the cross? How would you feel if you saw your sight-restorer done to death within five days, with fierce brutality?

I have to confess I do not know the answer to these questions but I suggest that none of us have appreciated the significance of this story about blind Bartimaeus until we have recognized how St Mark has set it as the last healing miracle that Jesus performed before he was crucified. What the gospel of St Mark is saying is that whatever may be the view we hold of Jesus of Nazareth – a superb teacher, a miracle worker, a reformer, even some kind of Messiah – we have not begun to understand him until we have eyes to see him on the cross at Jerusalem. Jesus is the *crucified* Messiah. He is our deliverer when we see what his death means. May God open our eyes.

15. The Demonstration

John 12.12–15 (NEB)   *The next day the great body of pilgrims who had come to the festival, hearing that Jesus was on the way to Jerusalem, took palm branches and went out to meet him, shouting, 'Hosanna! Blessings on him who comes in the name of the Lord! God bless the king of Israel!' Jesus found a donkey and mounted it, in accordance with the text of Scripture: 'Fear no more, daughter of Zion; see, your king is coming, mounted on an ass's colt.'*

Those of us who have lived in Central London these last ten or twenty years have grown weary of demonstrations and 'demos' as they have come to be called. Scarcely a weekend has seemed to pass without long slow-moving processions straggling through the streets. They display slogans on home-made placards lifted high proclaiming their protest, and punctuating the steady shuffle of feet with sudden, sharp, staccato shouts. Patiently the police plod dumbly beside them, and less patiently, and somewhat less dumbly, frustrated motorists wait for the blocked road to clear, cursing at time wasted and appointments missed.

Was it like this on the road to Jerusalem on the day we have come to call Palm Sunday, now celebrated in churches throughout the world wherever Christians meet for worship? Was it a kind of 'demo'? We commonly label it the triumphal entry of Jesus into Jerusalem. Was it a triumph? What sort of triumph?

1. The popularity of Jesus

The fourth gospel in telling this story is at pains to stress the popularity of Jesus. It extended right as far as this Sunday. It had been triggered off at the outset of his ministry by his miracles of healing, sustained all along and elevated to concert pitch by the raising of Lazarus from the grave at the end. And if the fourth gospel alone records this stupendous event St Luke accounts for the popularity of Jesus as due to 'all the mighty works (Greek 'powers') they had seen'. He also tells us that some Pharisees in the crowd were so incensed by this adulation that they even besought Jesus to reprimand his disciples for taking part. There is more: the fourth gospel describes how the Pharisees said one to another 'You see you are doing no good at all; why, all the world has gone after him.'

I draw attention to this popularity because I think Dorothy L. Sayers got it right in her play *The Man Born to be King* (Gollancz, 1944), when she said Jesus did not organize this demonstrative event himself. To think so would be completely out of character. Jesus never sought publicity in his ministry. What happened on this Palm Sunday was a *spontaneous* outburst of enthusiasm. The people organized it, in so far as it can be called organized at all. Listen again to the way the fourth gospel puts it. 'The next day the great body of pilgrims who had come to the festival, hearing that Jesus was on the way to Jerusalem, took palm branches and went out to meet him, shouting 'Hosanna! Blessings on him who comes in the name of the Lord! God bless the king of Israel!' Then Jesus found the donkey (the Greek has 'little donkey') and mounted it.

Before we analyse this popularity of Jesus we ought to take it as it stands. It really is extraordinary how this man born in obscurity and killed in ignominy on the town's dump heap with only a teaching ministry of three years, if that, who wrote nothing and of whom there is no indication what he looked like – it really is extraordinary, I say, that 'Jesus of Nazareth is the most widely revered figure in human history' (as the *Radio Times* expressed it on 6 January 1984). Why, even the London West End stage found something out of which to make 'a musical'! Let us admit it, Jesus is attractive still, even in our modern, materialistic, secular world. There is no lack of people ready to raise at least two cheers on his behalf. The fact really is remarkable. We ought first to take it just as it stands.

2. *Superficiality*

But why did Jesus accept this adulation if it is out of character? It may sound trite but I believe it to be profoundly true that he did so because he knew the pleasure it would give to people. They loved waving those palm branches! They loved spreading their garments in the roadway! They loved shouting their heads off! It was fun. Look into your own heart and mind. Don't you love a spectacle? Don't you turn out for a royal procession? Aren't you at least 'glued' to the television screen? It does us good to 'let go' on these public occasions. It does the public good. This is what I want to say first. Jesus knew this fact of human nature. God knows it. We must not let any misguided puritanical notions cheat us of this pleasant thought that God likes his people to enjoy themselves.

There is, however, more to Jesus's acquiescence in this popular acclaim on Palm Sunday than goodnaturedness. All along he 'kept a low profile' (as we say these days) because all too quickly the crowds ran to false conceptions about the Messiahship they might sense in him; and it was not easy to conceal the concept of Messiahship altogether. They however thought of Messiahship in terms of national ascendency, military prowess, their enemies licking the dust and a good time to be had by all. This was certainly not what Jesus came to bring. This was not the kind of Messiahship he embodied. But, however seriously the general public harboured these ideas, in a matter of days they would know how wrong they were. Pilate, the Roman governor would despatch Jesus as he would any other awkward public figure. And Jesus would not hit back. Furthermore when the bystanders saw him impaled on that gibbet they felt betrayed, bewildered, bitter, blasphemous – God knows what they felt! Jesus knew on Palm Sunday what was coming. He knew there was no danger now in letting even false notions of Messiahship have their fling. The truth would soon be out. Indeed at the end of the triumphal ride into Jerusalem all Jesus did was to look round the temple. What sort of Messiah is this? Had he not already given a hint by riding into Jerusalem on a little donkey? Did he look like the usual kind of conqueror?

So, superficial enthusiasm had its fling that day, but it did not last long. It couldn't. It never does.

3. Our demonstration today

Nevertheless we still observe Palm Sunday. We sing our Hosannas today. Palm crosses are distributed in many churches to the members of the congregations, and if there is any decoration in the church at all, as Holy Week begins, it is with palm branches purchased and kept for this annual occasion.

Our demonstration is different from that on the road to Jerusalem when Jesus rode that 'little donkey'. It has to be. We see a suffering Messiah. We see a king who does not elevate himself above people but who stoops to the lowest of the low, dying at last in the company of convicted terrorists, spat on and reviled. We do not see a Christ who has come to lift us out of all our difficulties and solve all our problems. Our Saviour does not save us out of our sorrows but through our sorrows. We are not made better beings by being cushioned all the way. We are made better by acquiring the inspiration and the stiffening to hack a way through our many trials and frequent tribulations. So, on this Palm Sunday we do not shout our Hosannas to one who 'got away from it all', but to one who went through it all himself. He saves us by sustaining us and he sustains us when we put our trust in him to do it. For remember he is the Lord. He is not simply the man from Nazareth. We are not waving flags to a mere human hero today but bowing the knee to the Divine, powerful in his assumed weakness. He has saved us. He will save us. So, we take up the shouts of the Galileans and Judaeans lining the road to Jerusalem that first Palm Sunday, 'Hosanna', Save now; and with less superficiality. For we see Jesus from this side of Good Friday. And we can be sure of this, God rejoices in our rejoicing. He always does. Did not St Paul write in Romans 12

'Rejoice with those who do rejoice'? Therefore with a full heart let us sing our praises –

> Sing, my tongue, the glorious battle
> Sing the last, the dread affray;
> O'er the Cross, the Victor's trophy,
> Sound the high triumphal lay,
> How, the pains of death enduring,
> Earth's Redeemer won the day.

Bishop Venantius Fortunatus
Tr. J. M. Neale and Compilers (AM)

16. Hurting and Healing

Matthew 21.14 (RSV) *'And the blind and the lame came to him in the temple, and he healed them.'*

About twenty years ago, although it only seems like yesterday, I was travelling with my wife by car into London along the A23, a road we have used hundreds of times. On the Croydon bypass, the A23 at Waddon Marsh rises and curves at the same time as it crosses a railway bridge. The night was dark and very wet, the road slippery. An oncoming car braked heavily, skidded across the road and crashed into us. We were not badly hurt, though the car was in a mess. Even now, after all this time, I invariably drive over that bridge warily. I remember it as a place where we got hurt.

1. Hurting

The Jerusalem temple in Jesus's day had become a place of hurting for many of the pilgrims who visited it at the great festivals and they treated it warily. This ought never to have been. What happened was that worshippers came up from Galilee, Hebron or some other provincial place, bringing their lamb or pigeon to offer as their personal sacrifice in the temple as the law enjoined. They knew they needed to have it checked before being allowed to offer it, because only the unblemished was acceptable. A cunning scrupulosity however contrived to reject many of the offerings, cunning because then the wretched pilgrims must needs visit the temple shop in order to purchase certified offerings at fancy prices, so lining someone's pocket. So these cheated pilgrims came to look upon the temple as a house of God turned into a place of merchandise where sincere and simple people got hurt.

The Alternative Service Book has chosen the passage of scripture which records this to be read at a church's Dedication Festival. It seems a strange choice till the point is grasped that Jesus turned this place of hurting into a place of healing, which is what every church should be – a place of healing because of Christ's real presence in it.

This is what happened. There came a day (the synoptic gospels say at the close of his ministry) when Jesus strode into the temple, made straight for the shop and before anyone was sufficiently aware of what was happening, tipped over the shopkeepers' counters setting free the captive pigeons. There never was such a scrabbling on the temple floor after the scattered coins, or such a flapping of wings. Tempers of course rose. Voices were raised, but Jesus shouted back, 'My house shall be called a house of prayer; but you make it a den of robbers'. And if I understand human nature aright my guess is that the throng of unwilling customers chuckled grimly behind cupped hands at the shopkeepers' discomfiture. It is what they had wanted to cause, but did not dare. And of course it wasn't long before Jesus paid for his daring.

2. Healing

The immediate sequel, however, was entirely different as St Matthew recorded it. 'And the blind and the lame came to Jesus in the temple, and he healed them.' So the place of hurting became through Jesus's presence the place of healing.

A man does not need to have been a parish priest for very long to discover how many there are in every congregation who have come there in the first place because they have been hurt in life. Not hurt by the Church itself as the temple once hurt its worshippers, though in its history, ancient and modern, occasions have not been wanting where sensitive souls have been severely hurt by the harsh, narrow and uncaring attitude meted out to them by the Church on account of their sins and misfortunes. But, where there has been a ministry after the pattern of Christ's breadth of compassion for people, there have crept in those who cannot see any sense in what has happened to them in their lives and who limp along because of the severe blows it has dealt them, being in this sense blind and lame. They have come in hope of healing.

It is well for every local church to be reminded that it should be a place of healing. It should be a place where men and women suffering from the burden of some particular wrongdoing can 'get it off their chests' and receive the divine forgiveness. Here if anywhere the work of a faithful, compassionate and wise priest comes into his own. Here healing of the human spirit can begin. No church is fulfilling its purpose unless it is felt to be a place where all can be told, guarded in secrecy for ever, and then the forgiveness of God will wash its stains away leaving the penitent clean for all eternity.

Spiritual healing may need to take various forms. Sin is not the only blind and crippling factor in life. There is misunderstanding, a sense of personal inadequacy, loneliness that eats into the heart, and fear of the unknown future. In all these cases the Church is there to heal. Nor is healing of the body necessarily outside the scope of its ministry. Far more illnesses than has hitherto been realized owe their origin to some spiritual malady or deformity. Our modern appreciation of the essential wholeness of the human personality, what is often called the psychosomatic approach, has opened up a ministry of physical healing (not in competition with the medical profession) which has been neglected too long.

A church should be a place of healing, spiritual and physical, of those who have been hurt in life if it is to live and work after the mind of the Lord and Master.

3. Prayer

And now prayer. When Jesus overturned the merchants' counters in the temple and released the captive pigeons causing havoc by the suddenness and severity of his action he called out, 'My house shall be called a house of prayer'.

It could, I think, be justly claimed that there has been a welcome revival in contemporary Church life of the practice of prayer. For a decade and more now there has been a steady stream of books published about prayer, how to pray and what to pray. Christian prayer is more than meditation, considered to be psychologically beneficial in a tense and hurrying world. It is putting ourselves, our aspirations and our needs, and those about whom we are concerned, consciously into the beneficent will of God.

There is a sense in which intercessory prayer is the heart of Christian prayer and the point at which it becomes most inexplicable, and yet we are bidden 'to make our requests known unto God'. Jesus was a man of prayer, couching all his prayers in thanksgiving, as should we all. He prayed at the crisis times of his life, notably his baptism, transfiguration, and agony in the garden of Gethsemene before his arrest by the temple police. He prayed before some momentous decisive action had to be taken, like the choosing of his twelve disciples. He prayed alone out in the open before the day's work began, and one night he continued all night in prayer. He prayed too for individuals; he prayed for Peter that his faith should not fail.

We cannot tell God what he should do in any situation. We cannot provide him with information of which he is not aware. Nevertheless by putting ourselves and our concerns in his hands and by uniting with others in doing so, that is causing the whole Church of God to pray, we are opening avenues along which the power of God to heal is able to operate. And we must persist in our praying, not in order to keep God goaded into action, but to keep ourselves in the line of his gracious will, making his action possible in our situation. Prayer is opening the door for God to enter.

'My house shall be called a house of prayer.' What a gauge these words become to test the worth of any and every local church.

Conclusion

We come back to that Jerusalem temple, defiled as Jesus saw it by the tricky merchandise that was carried on in its precincts. By a symbolic act he cleansed it, infuriating the priests by his unwarranted (as they saw it) assumption of authority. But as St Matthew saw it, his action, far from being that of an outsider breaking in, was in fact the rightful owner taking over. He shouted out 'My house shall be called a house of prayer'. '*My* house' mark you! And when the rightful owner was really present then the lame and the blind came groping and hobbling in, only to march out running and jumping, for they were gloriously healed. The place of hurting had become the place of healing, on account of Jesus's presence. What a difference when the real presence of Christ is consciously experienced in our churches, dedicated to his worship! Miracles take place, miracles of healing.

17. The Garment of Gratitude

Matthew 22.12   *'Friend, how camest thou in hither not having a wedding garment?'*

1. The generous invitation

'Friend, how camest thou in hither?' The obvious answer is in through the door! How else would you expect him to come in? Up the drain pipe? or the fire escape at the back? No, he walked in large as life through the front door. What is more, the ushers didn't stop him. They couldn't stop him. He showed them his invitation card. 'HM The King requests the pleasure of the company of Joseph Bloggs at the marriage of his son and to the banquet afterwards at the palace.' As soon as he passed through the entrance hall however the ushers held up their hands in horror. They had observed his clothes. They couldn't help observing his clothes. Courduroy trousers and a tee-shirt! Everyone else was in morning dress or uniform, and the ladies in long dresses. But what could the ushers do? They watched him make his way to the seating plan, find his place at the table and then sit down, nonchalance written all over his face.

Then it happened. It was the dreaded moment. The doors at the end of the banqueting hall were thrown open. The trumpeters in the gallery played a rousing fanfare. The guests rose to their feet. They clapped their hands as the royal procession made its way to the top table. But the King did not immediately sit down although the flunkey had pushed back his chair. He looked over the guests. He saw the man in the corduroy trousers and the tee-shirt. In that glittering assembly you couldn't help seeing him. And then, while everyone held their breath, the King strode down the gangway between the tables and said to the man in a loud voice everyone could hear, 'Friend, how comest thou hither not having a wedding garment?' And since no reply was forthcoming, he said to his servants, 'Bind him hand and foot, and take him away, and cast him into outer darkness; there shall be weeping and gnashing of teeth.'

2. Identifying the stranger

And you say 'What a fantastic story! Nothing like this could possibly happen!' Couldn't it? Or you say, 'What a silly fuss about clothes! What does it matter what we wear?' But clothes are the first rough and ready index of the kind of person the wearer is. Ask those who sit on selection boards. Don't they note first the appearance of the various applicants for the job on offer? Or maybe you attempt to defend the man in his corduroy trousers and tee-shirt and say 'Perhaps he couldn't afford a morning coat. After all they cost money and even the hiring fee isn't trifling.' Or next you say 'Perhaps he had just come in from the fields and hadn't time to change'. But you notice the man when charged had no one word of excuse on the grounds of poverty or any other. He had in fact nothing to say.

Who is this man at the royal banquet sticking out in that company like a sore thumb? The devastating thought is – it could be you, it could be me.

This is the permanently awkward fact about Jesus's parables and why some of his hearers stopped their ears. They don't stay outside as stories. They worm their way inside the hearer's conscience raising subtle and disturbing questions. Jesus actually (according to St Matthew) told this parable when, almost at the very end of his ministry, he was engaged in a battle royal with the chief priests and Pharisees. They knew he was charging them with having turned down God's invitation to fellowship with him. There was even a subtle reference to the Gentiles accepting what the Jews refused. Gross ingratitude was his accusation. But the charge cannot only be laid at the door of nations but at the door of individuals, whether Jew or Gentile. So the pin-pointing of the man without a wedding garment. It could be you. It could be me.

3. Our eucharistic banquet

You see, what we have going on here in the church this morning at this Parish Communion is a sacramental replay of that royal banquet. We are all invited. There never was such an open invitation to any banquet, for you must understand that what is being offered here is nothing less than the gift of eternal life, now and in the world to come, open to us through the death and resurrection of our Lord Jesus Christ. What an offer! What an opportunity! And it is open to all without condition of sex, colour, rank, class, occupation, income group – and what is most surprising of all – even moral status. The good and the bad receive an invitation card. 'Come, for all things are now ready.'

And some tear it up and put it in the waste-paper basket. A few are so incensed they 'take it out' on the bearer of the invitation which could be the postman, just as if that would do any good. And off they go to the farm, the shop, the golf club or the task of mowing the lawn or cleaning the car. They think no more about it.

4. Ingratitude

But not one man. O no! Not one man! He is not quite so easy to understand at first. He looks at the invitation card. He hears the word of the gospel, 'God so loved the world that he gave his only begotten Son that whosoever believeth in him should not perish but have eternal life.' And he says to himself 'That isn't much of a gospel. There is something in it I suppose, but think of the scallywags you'll let in if you start giving invitations like this to all and sundry. Surely you must hedge the invitations around a bit.'

'Take me for instance. I've lived a good life. I haven't fiddled my income tax returns. I haven't fooled around with sex. I have given pretty generously to charities. Come to think of it, God jolly well ought to take me in and others like me.'

And so there is no gratitude in this man's heart at all for the gospel, and that is why he does not bother to turn up at the wedding feast in the morning coat (which he possesses all right). He doesn't reckon the occasion merits it. And just to show what a poor view he takes of the party, he'll turn up in his corduroys and tee-shirt.

5. Further identification

A moment ago in seeking to identify this oddity at the banqueting table I said, it could be you, it could be me *at this Eucharist*. No, not literally, I am wearing no tee-shirt, not even under these vestments. And you have come suitably dressed. But we could lack the *garment of gratitude*. We could have come along with the idea in our heads that we are most suitable, without any need of dressing up to be recipients of God's offer of eternal salvation in Jesus Christ our Lord. It is so easy for us, good Church people – and let there be no misunderstanding, we need good Church people, they are worthy of all honour, indeed I think they are the backbone of our country – but it is so easy for us to slip into the frame of mind which reckons that God owes us a place in his eternal kingdom. And he doesn't. But he offers it to us for nothing. What is required of us is to put out our hands to receive, and to do so trustingly, just as we shall do physically in a moment in the

Eucharist. It is the same for all of us, which is why we shall all kneel side by side without distinction. And however old we are, however young, however experienced in the Christian life, however inexperienced, the basis is always the same. We receive the life eternal from God as a gift we do not earn. So the garment of thanksgiving is the proper one. This whole service is called the Eucharist, the thanksgiving, lest we forget.

I come back to the banquet which celebrated the marriage of the King's son and see the King striding down the tables to turn out the wretched man in his corduroys and tee-shirt. Are you sorry for him? You ought to be. You ought to be sorry for all who do not recognize the marvellous offer God makes to us, because life in default of that offer is dark. We must try to get him in. This is what the Church is for – to get people into God's eternal kingdom.

18. Questioning Jesus

Mark 12.13 (NEB) *A number of Pharisees and men of Herod's party were sent to trap him with a question.*

I wonder if there was ever a time more than the present when questions were asked of almost everybody and everything. I am not thinking of the Socratic method of teaching or of the enquiring mind which betokens intelligence. I am thinking of Sir Robin Day putting some politician through his paces. I am thinking of the BBC sound radio programme on Friday evenings entitled 'Any Questions'. I am thinking of the press reporters who come crowding round someone whose house has been burgled, someone just rescued from drowning, someone torn with grief over a bereavement or a kidnapping. 'How did you feel when this happened to you?' Questions can be cruel. Some are meant to be cruel. Information is *not* what is being sought. They are meant to hurt, to expose and to trap. Jesus got caught in this rough procedure. Towards the end of his ministry from all sides he was pestered with questions. My text represents only one occasion, but it gives the flavour. 'A number of Pharisees and men of Herod's party were sent to trap him with a question.'

Let us listen to some of their questions. Then we shall see where they thought he was vulnerable and where, in their opinion, justification existed for bringing him down.

1. Divorce

One of the first was on the divorce question. This was a hot potato; still is. I do not think the questioners on this occasion had the slightest interest in what were Jesus's views on this subject, any more than thousands of people have today. That is to say, no interest to the extent of making any attempt to live by what he taught on the subject. What governs attitudes in this matter for the most part is not principle but public opinion. Those who put the question (St Matthew says it was the Pharisees) reckoned they had him nicely in their grasp. There were two views current on the divorce question. One was the liberal view following Rabbi Hillel, the other was the conservative view following Shammai. With the former a man could divorce his wife, for instance, for being an indifferent cook. With the latter, there had to be compliance with Mosaic regulations. So they put their question, 'Is it lawful for a man to divorce his wife?' or, as St Matthew has it, 'Is it lawful for a man to divorce his wife on any and every ground?' They waited. With whom would he side? Hillel the liberal or Shammai the strict? What he did was to side with neither but go behind both, to God's original intention in the creation of male and female. 'What God has joined together, man must not separate.' This is *not* what his questioners wished to hear. But then who does? Is this a justifiable ground for rejecting Jesus of Nazareth?

2. Authority

Another day Jesus was walking in the temple court, when the chief priests, lawyers and elders made straight for him – a powerful deputation. Clearly they meant business. They had a question ready. 'By what authority are you acting like this?, and as a supplementary, 'Who gave you authority to act in this way?' What was the trouble? No doubt one incident in particular, that masterful ejection from the temple of the money-changers and dealers in pigeons, and his prohibition for the temple to be used as a short cut for carrying goods. But it was not only this event that galled them. It was the recognition by the people of the personal authority of a man who lacked official authorization. Self-authenticating authority, however, is very difficult to get at. It is simply no use asking a genius, Why are you a genius, or who gave you authority to be a genius? Such questions do not make sense. Since therefore the authority of Jesus partook of this class how was he to answer? What in fact he did was to put to his questioners a question. 'The baptism of John: was it from God or from man? Answer me.' And of course they found they couldn't. Neither therefore did Jesus answer the question they put to him. So there stood the authority of Jesus staring them in the face and they did not like it. It was another reason for bringing him down. And their reason still stands. Modern man hates being under authority. He wants freedom from every kind of restraint. Why should anyone ever suggest to him how he should conduct his life? The affront associated with Jesus is starkly explicit in the titles given him – Lord and Master. Have we not here another justifiable ground for rejecting him?

3. Political quietism

And then this business of paying taxes. I see one of our clergy has withheld part of his income tax, because he disagrees with the way the Government uses some of the money it collects for financing the nuclear deterrent. This kind of problem existed in Jesus's day. The Jews hated paying taxes to the Romans; not surprisingly, because the Romans had marched into their land, occupied all the key positions, posted soldiers next to the very temple itself spying on all they did; and you can be sure made free with the girls when they could catch them. Fancy paying for that! Should you pay taxes to a government with which you disagree and whose policies you abhor? What would Jesus say about the ethics of the situation? But the Pharisees and men of Herod's party (odd bedfellows, boding no good) were not particularly interested in Jesus's ethics. They were confident they possessed a winner of a trap question. Listen to their smarmy approach. 'Master, you are an honest man, we know, and truckle to no man, whoever he may be; you teach in all honesty the way of life that God requires.' (Yes, they laid it on with a trowel.) 'Are we or are we not permitted to pay taxes to the Roman Emperor?'. . . Just how could he get out of that one? If he said 'Yes', he was in trouble with the Jews. If he said 'No', he was in trouble with the Romans. But he was not trapped. He said, 'Pay Caesar what is due to Caesar, and pay God what is due to God.' And whatever are the respective spheres (and the argument has never ceased), it was clear Jesus was not going to lead a rebellion against the Romans. What use then was leadership if it did not espouse political revolution or even protest? So these men had no time for him. Is there not here another justifiable ground for rejecting Jesus?

4. Resurrection life

And one more question. The Sadducees concocted this one. They were the people who, among other things, reckoned that the notion of a resurrection life after death is plain silly. They reckoned they could derive fun from their question if they asked it in the hearing of the crowds, and slanted it on the subject of marriage, always good for a laugh. So their comic, if not bawdy story, designed to bring Jesus down by public ridicule since all else had failed. 'Master, Moses laid it down for us that if there are brothers, and one dies leaving a wife but no child, then the next should marry the widow and carry on his brother's family. Now there were seven brothers. The first took a wife and died without issue. Then the second married her, and he too died without issue. So did the third. Eventually the seven of them died, all without issue. Finally the woman died.' – Someone was bound to shout here, 'What a woman!' – And now the question. 'At the resurrection, when they come back to life, whose wife will she be, since all seven had married her?' Would Jesus have an answer? It came all right and with two strings attached. One a charge of ignorance of the Scriptures to which they had hitched their story; and two, a 'backhander' about resurrection life being like that of the angels in which the Sadducees prided themselves on *not* believing. This counter attack impressed a lawyer standing by. All the same the question of the reasonableness of the resurrection had not gone away. The Sadducees were rationalists. If religion means reasonable behaviour in the community fair enough, let us have religion. But if it requires belief in miracles contrary to natural law, angels, spirits and life after death, none of which is verifiable scientifically, then intelligence requires us to be rid of it and Jesus too if all these are involved.

So these four questions were designed to show up where Jesus is vulnerable. But the method failed. It even backfired. Jesus won the last cheer from the listening crowds which of course infuriated his opponents even more. They were mad to bring him down. And then their chance appeared. A traitor turned up. That story, however, must be left for another occasion. We are left with the question. Is Jesus vulnerable? Is he able to be wounded? (This is what 'vulnerable' means). The answer is 'Yes'. We Christians worship a wounded and crucified Christ. That, strange to say, at the end of the day is *the ground of his appeal*. Did his opponents think of such a possibility when they sought to wound him with their ensnaring questions? I doubt it. I doubt if they could have thought of it. I doubt if anyone could. It would be unthinkable had it not actually happened. Christ saves by his wounds, not by his ability to avoid the traps of his clever questioners bent on his destruction. Ours is a suffering Messiah. At the end of the day, we shall have to come round to this. *The cross* is the instrument of our salvation.

19. Three Sharp Warnings

Matthew 25.13 (NEB) '*Keep awake then; for you never know the day or the hour.*'

Do you think Jesus really uttered the three parables that comprise the whole of chapter 25 of St Matthew's gospel? Or could it be that St Matthew invented them himself? Did the early Church perhaps concoct them and put them in Jesus's mouth? Or was it that Jesus did produce three parables something like these but they have become distorted in transmission? And you say 'What is the trouble? Why are you making these suggestions? Well, look at the parables. Look at the climax to each one of them. First a shut door with five girls in the dark crying for admission. Then at the close of the second parable 'Fling the useless servant out into the dark, the place of wailing and grinding of teeth!' And thirdly, 'And they shall go away to eternal punishment but the righteousness will enter eternal life.' Are you surprised by my question 'Do you think Jesus really uttered these three parables?' Do they not sound too harsh to flow from the lips of Jesus? Or is it that our estimate of him is wrong? He was not as easy going as we have tended to imagine.

Before we go any further we ought to note where St Matthew has set these three parables in his gospel. They stand almost at the end, appearing between that daunting chapter on the destruction of Jerusalem, prefiguring the end of the world, and that solemn chapter which tells of Jesus's arrest and trial, with the story of Judas's betrayal at one end and Peter's denial at the other. The situation is comparable to a man buckling on his battle dress to stride out into some terrible conflict. The tension is high, nerves are taut; this is no time for easy-go. In what lies ahead everything could be lost. Is it surprising then that sharp warnings are given? What is at stake is the very survival of the faith itself. 'Be careful' says Jesus in effect 'you do not know when the attack will take place', or in the words of my text 'Keep awake then; for you never know the day or the hour'. What are these three warnings against being overtaken and losing the faith entirely?

1. Thoughtlessness

First the warning against thoughtlessness. It is possible to forfeit the life eternal by consistently being plain silly. And before any feminine wrath arises because the picture of silliness provided by the parable is of girls, let it be noted that the picture provided of prudence is also of girls. Girls can be wise and girls can be stupid. So can men. The point is, wherever thoughtlessness obtains there the risk of losing the life eternal is enormous.

This comes as something of a surprise. If an opinion poll were conducted among members of church congregations about what were reckoned to be the disqualifications for entry into the kingdom of God St Paul's words might be supplied by way of answer 'Make no mistake: no fornicator, or idolator, none who are guilty of either adultery or of homosexual perversion, no thieves or grabbers or drunkards or slanderers or swindlers will possess the kingdom of God' (1 Corinthians 6.9). Jesus, however, said by means of his parable, 'I will tell you how it will be when the kingdom of God is a present reality; a number of people will miss it altogether for no other reason than that they were plain silly, they didn't think, they were lightweights, flibbertigibbets'.

We need this warning. We need it because it is most unlikely that many Church people will be involved in the misadventures St Paul listed for the benefit of the Corinthians. So we might feel ourselves eminently qualified to say, 'I'm all right Jack', completely forgetting that we can forfeit the whole bundle of the blessings of faith in Christ crucified and risen simply by being plain silly, by thoughtlessness and not giving our minds to the offer which the gospel makes to us.

2. Laziness

The picture Jesus painted to illustrate the danger of thoughtlessness consisted of five silly girls who failed to provide sufficient oil to keep their lamps burning should the wedding procession after dark be long in putting in an appearance. The picture he painted to illustrate laziness consisted of three men each provided with capital to get going in some business enterprise and one went and buried his. The day of reckoning came, as it always does. Two of the three had substantial profits to show for their labours, the third only engaged in sufficient work to dig a hole for his money when he was given it and sufficient work to dig it up again when the boss returned. For that he earned the rebuke 'You lazy rascal!' By way of excuse he complained that he knew his master to be a hard man, which allegation was not refuted. It even constituted an added reason for energy. And the hardness did not, in the event, appear to be an inaccurate description of the master's character; for he demanded that the lazy man forfeit even the little he had and the energetic man be compensated further by being allocated what this third man had lost.

Maybe this warning against laziness comes as a surprise that as the warning against thoughtlessness. It suggests that we have to work for our salvation, work to qualify for eternal life, and everyone with only half a notion of the gospel of Christ must know that we cannot work for it at all because it is a gift through Jesus Christ, free and unmerited. What, then, is this counsel for energetic enterprise? What is this warning against lazy inaction?

It comes lest we should make no effort whatever to *propagate* our faith; and if this word 'propagate' sounds too grand to fit our condition let me break it down. It is possible to stay satisfied that we have been baptized. We are therefore Christians; what more is required? There are those who were confirmed in their 'teens and their first communion turned out in practice to be their last. It is not rare to encounter men and women who make no effort at all to keep the local church standing, but who would be the first to argue that this is a Christian country and that contempt for law and general disorderliness is scandalous. What have they done to see that the Christian faith has its witnesses in brick and stone in the land, let alone in its living agents? And I have said nothing about standing up for faith when we hear it ridiculed. All these inactivities, including slackness over Sunday worship, are the inactivities that constitute the laziness which causes us to forfeit the benefits with which we have been endowed by the grace of God.

Surely we know that if we fail to exercise one of our physical limbs it will become physically atrophied. The same holds true of our spiritual endowments. We shall lose them if we do not use them. Then will follow the awful rebuke of the Lord Christ – 'You lazy rascal!' No, we dislike this tough speech; but, according to the way St Matthew has arranged the materials in his gospel, this is how Jesus spoke towards the end of his life. These three parables represent almost the climax of his public teaching.

3. Lovelessness

And now this third parable, commonly called 'the sheep and the goats'. We know it so well. Has it not, with the best will in the world, almost suffered from over-exposure by those agencies and individuals commendably concerned for the amelioration of the conditions suffered by the disabled, dispossessed, incarcerated and impoverished, notably in the 'third world'? Basically the parable comes as a warning that we shall lose our faith if we lack brotherly love in practical action.

And this surprises us again. We do not reckon with the battle for what we believe in being joined in the field of action as well as in the sphere of intellect. Surely our religion is in jeopardy if we cannot defend it in argument. Possibly. The greater danger by far, however, lies in the realm of lovelessness. The Christian religion begins in love. 'God so loved the world that he gave.' Love in action. And with us it must operate first at home, in the family, in the office, in the supermarket, in the political arena, across class barriers and across racial barriers *in the next street*. Lovelessness at home coupled with love for the underprivileged abroad is a travesty, and the consequence is the gradual shrinkage of Christian faith and discipleship till there is nothing left. The Catholic creeds without love are of little worth. Love of our fellows in need is not a substitute for faith but faith without love has defected on the field of battle. It is already dead.

Conclusion

'Keep awake then; for you never know the day or the hour.' Three enemies are crouching at the house of our faith waiting to pounce and destroy. They may not look deadly but they are. So three warnings. *First* against thoughtlessness. Are we giving our minds to our religion? When did we last read a serious book to help build up a reserve of knowledge of what we believe? The five foolish girls were caught napping because they carried no reserve of oil for their lamps. *Secondly* laziness. What effort are we putting into our Christian profession? Perhaps we are growing slack about worship? *Thirdly* lovelessness. Without knowing it we are saying to ourselves, 'I'm all right Jack'; perhaps we are; but we won't be all right for long if we do not go out of our way to help people, and better still, to become 'helping people' unaware of the good we are doing, so much has it become part of our nature. Then we are safe in the kingdom of God. So keep awake. Let the whole Church keep awake.

20. The Last Supper

St Luke 22.15 (NEB)   *'How I have longed to eat this Passover with you before my death.'*

1. *Expressing and cementing fellowship*

You will not expect me on this Maundy Thursday, and certainly not at the Eucharist, to speak of anything but the last supper (as we have come to call it) which Jesus shared with his disciples. You must not imagine that such a supper was a rare occasion. Jesus had been constantly sharing meals with these twelve men throughout his ministry; and not only with them. Time and time again he accepted invitations out to meals as I have indicated in another sermon.

Eating with people was a *significant* act among the Jews. It still is with the Arabs too. You do not of course sit down to a meal with your enemy. And in India the caste system leaves no doubt as to those with whom you may, and may not, eat. Eating together is a powerful sign in all these cultures of affinity, of closeness, or brotherhood. We ought to note this as we listen to Jesus's words, as St Luke presents them, 'How I have longed to eat this Passover with you before my death'.

Perhaps we might try to picture the scene. We shall need to empty our minds of Leonardo da Vinci's representation painted on the refectory wall of Santa Maria delle Grazie in Milan. The original supper was not held in some graceful hall lending its lines to the display of an artist's mastery of symmetry and perspective. Jesus assembled with his disciples in the upper room of a two-storied house, unusual if only because the house consisted of two stories instead of the usual one. And this upper room was large. It would need to be to accommodate thirteen men to a sit-down meal. And it was sit-down because for the Jews a stand-up buffet supper, or a Scandinavian Smörgasbord would be unthinkable. Half the point of the meal was for the host and his guests to relax in each other's company.

Influenced by Greek customs at this period the guests would recline on sofas on the left elbow eating with the right hand. There would be no knives and forks, but plates and wine cups. The food would be placed in a central dish on the table and it was the custom of the host to hand the most tasty portion to the guest he most wished to honour, dipping their hands together in the dish. How all the other guests took from the dish thereafter was regulated by strict rules of etiquette.

The disciples would expect the occasion to be a merry one. The singing of the four psalms called 'The Great Hallel' was meant to 'raise the roof ' at the Passover feast. An apocryphal gospel called *The Acts of John* tells of the disciples making a ring round Jesus, their host, and dancing. The whole occasion lent itself to an expression and cementing of warm brotherliness, signifying a close bond of unity.

2. *The Passover*

When was the last supper held? Yes, it was Thursday, but was it the thirteenth or the fourteenth of the Jewish month Nisan? Scholars write long and intricate arguments about this. Was Jesus celebrating the Passover or was he anticipating it by twenty-four hours? The arguments arise from the fact that the first three gospels clearly designate the meal as the Passover meal – 'How I have longed to eat this Passover with you before my death' (Luke 22.15) – whereas the fourth gospel makes the crucifixion of Jesus fall on Passover Day, that is Friday Nisan 14.

You would not wish me to use this present time of worship to work over these arguments. Those who have the inclination could read them in a book by Jeremias called *The Eucharistic Words of Jesus*. Suffice it to say, that I shall follow the chronology of the fourth gospel here and take the view that Jesus with his last supper anticipated the Jewish Passover by one day. He kept it on Nisan 13.

Whichever view on this matter is taken, however, the last supper *was Jesus's Passover*. That is to say, it cannot be understood apart from the Passover described in the Book of Exodus. That feast, though very ancient, came to be inseparably associated with the deliverance of the Hebrew people from their slavery in Egypt under an alien power. And not only that, but with the beginning of Israel's nationhood and with the solemn covenant when the Hebrews pledged themselves as God's chosen people to do his will.

All the ritual acts of the Passover festival kept every year in Jewish homes looked back to that epoch-making event called the Exodus. It is true that by the time of Jesus the participants had ceased to eat the meal standing up as if ready for flight, recalling the haste with which they ate that last meal in Egypt, but the unleavened bread was still eaten and the two cups of wine drunk with tiny sips of salt and water in between in memory of the tears shed in Egypt's grim servitude. Psalm 114 recalling the story of the Exodus was recited, after which the sacrificial lamb was eaten along with bitter herbs, then two more cups of wine, followed by the singing of the Great Hallel, that is Psalms 113–118 beginning 'Praise the Lord, ye servants: O praise the name of the Lord'.

This then was the setting, this was the mood of the meal in which Jesus at the last supper took bread, blessed it and said 'This is my body'. The Exodus dominated the minds of all present when he went on to take a cup of wine, offer thanks to God and then give it to all present; 'This is my blood of the covenant shed for many' ('many' is a Hebrew way of saying 'for all'). Can there be any doubt? Jesus was accomplishing a new exodus. Had not St Luke already used this word of Jesus's death when he recounted the transfiguration scene? Jesus was also sealing a new covenant in his own blood. The last supper, I say, cannot be understood, apart from the Passover.

3. The sacrificial death

And now I wish to say that not only cannot the last supper be understood without looking back and connecting it with the Jewish Passover, it cannot be understood without looking forward and connecting it with the crucifixion which followed the next day. The Passover, the last supper and the death of Jesus are all three inextricably bound together. They are three parts of the redeeming act of God.

And so the last supper has entered into the life *and work* of the Christian Church. We do it in remembrance of him who asked that we should. Basically it was a farewell supper. Final farewells are terrible. The time and the place get stamped on the mind. This was a *last* supper.

In a moving book called *The House on Prague Street* (Wm Allen & Co., 1981), Hana Demetz, the authoress, tells of her mother bidding farewell to her house where her parents and grandparents had lived before her and which was so much a part of her own life. She sensed what the issue would be for the Jews, now that the Nazis had occupied Czechoslovakia. So, taking her daughter's hand, she went slowly through each room of the house beginning in the cellar. When she came to the bedroom she laid her hands gently on the great grandparents' double bed, and the blue flowered bowl and the soap-pot her grandmother used. Then into the maids' room and finally through an iron door into the attic, where they sat side by side for a while on the old trousseau chest. The mother did not speak. And the daughter did not understand; but later she did. Her mother had been saying farewell to the house and all that had entered through it into her life. Not long afterwards soldiers saw that she left for a concentration camp.

The last supper was the last. 'When the time came', wrote St Luke, 'he took his place at table, and the apostles with him; and he said to them, "How I have longed to eat this Passover with you before my death!"' Next day that death came in almost the most cruel form possible – crucifixion. And while the soldiers were nailing him there, all the Jewish households were making the final preparations for their Passover lambs to be killed and the festival kept, celebrating the deliverance from the bondage of slavery in Egypt. It was Nisan 14. And on that cross the Lamb of God was being slain to free us from all that holds us down and holds us back from fellowship with God and he with us.

O yes, I am theologizing now, but what will you have me do? Trace step by step the way in which this interpretation of Jesus's death came to find its place in the New Testament? Time and place forbid, but there are two points of vital significance for us, and I mean vital. One is that since the Passover, last supper and crucifixion are bound together, we partake of the benefits of God's redemptive acts as we partake in faith of that last supper repeated in our Eucharists today. Jesus meant it to be so. This is why he took bread and broke it. This is why he poured out wine and they all ate and drank in his presence. We partake of the benefits of his passion when we take part in faith in this Eucharist. The action is life imparting. It is vital.

And the second point is this. That last supper was held in order to express and cement the fellowship of Christ's disciples among themselves. The Eucharist does so still. We are here because we all alike are beneficiaries of his sacrifice. So we kneel together side by side without distinction of rank, class, colour, income bracket, or sex. And we kneel humbly. We do not argue here. We do not even ask questions. We say nothing at all, except perhaps 'Amen'. All we do is hold out our hands to receive. We do it together in gratitude. 'Thanks be to God for his unspeakable gift.'

21. Gethsemane

Mark 14.32 (NEB) *When they reached a place called Geth-semane, he said to his disciples, 'Sit here while I pray'.*

I wish I did not have to preach this sermon. I wish I could avoid the incident that has come to be called 'Gethsemane' altogether. I doubt if I am the man for it. I doubt if I possess the verbal skills, the spiritual sensitivity or the theological insight to portray this most moving and indeed most authentic scene in all the gospel records. For this is a certainty, believers or unbelievers in Christ alike have almost to a man admitted that here we are dealing with what actually happened. The narrative in St Mark, the source of St Matthew's and St Luke's accounts as well, bears all the indications of authenticity and could well have derived from St Peter's reminiscences. With what consummate delicacy and poignancy the story is told! And who but St Peter would have cast the disciples in such a poor light? I wish I did not have to preach this sermon. But what can I do? It is here, and nowhere else, that we come closer to the man Jesus. If I leave out Gethsemane, I shall fail to show Jesus as he was.

1. The scene itself

First we must picture the scene. Gethsemane is an ordinary word, meaning 'oil press'. Close to Jerusalem's eastern wall, beyond the brook Kidron, was an enclosed property, a garden, probably deriv-ing its name from an oil press. Immediately after the last supper Jesus with eleven disciples (Judas had defected by then) made for this garden, perhaps a place Jesus frequently used for private prayer. There was a full moon. The stillness of the night would be broken by the swirl of the brook Kidron and the sharp staccato shouts of the Roman sentries up on the tower of Antonia overlook-ing the temple area.

Leaving eight disciples possibly at the entrance of the garden,

Jesus went further in taking Peter, James and John, three intimates of his. All at once has was overcome in mind and spirit. St Mark's description employs strong words. He writes of 'horror and dismay' which apparently Jesus was powerless to conceal. 'My heart is ready to break with grief;' he said to his disciples, 'stop here, and stay awake'. Then going forward, St Luke's says 'a stone's throw', the three saw what must have astonished and alarmed them. Their consistently calm Master threw himself on the ground – St Matthew says 'on his face' – and agonizingly pleaded with his Father, breaking out into strong crying and tears (Hebrews 5.7) that if it were possible he might be delivered even at this eleventh hour from the terrible conflict about to begin. St Luke (a medical man) mentions how the intensity of his anguish was so sharp his sweat fell from his face like drops of blood. The disciples had never seen anything to compare. On and on the agonizing storm went. Twice he came back to the now sleeping disciples for human companionship but none was to be had.

In any case it was too late. All at once armed men with swords and cudgels burst into the garden. Torches lit up their faces and that of the man leading the party – it was Judas. One of the disciples made a futile attempt at resistance with a sword but there was no need. Jesus, consummately calm again, walked towards the intruders and gave himself up. The disciples saw in a flash how hopeless was their situation and made their escape while the going was good. The soldiers made a grab at one young man on the run; so anxious was he to make his getaway he left his clothes in the hands of his would-be captor. Meanwhile the squad of soldiers secured their prisoner and marched him back into the city.

2. Close to us

The scene is terrible but it brings Jesus very close to us. It simply is not possible after watching it to think of him as a kind of heavenly being *masquerading* as a mortal man. Jesus was a mortal man. Those nails the soldiers would drive into his hands and feet would hurt. That cruel whip with leaden spikes threaded into its leather thongs which some Roman would lift off its hook and apply with fury to Jesus's back, in the yard at the back of Pilate's lodging, would draw blood, red blood. That rough hewn lumbering cross which he would be forced to lug along the via Dolorosa would be too heavy, he would crumple under it. Here was no superman upon whom violence could make no kind of dent but someone you could kill, and kill slowly if you wished to pile on the cruelty.

And Jesus had feelings like us. Are we not all tempted to cross our bridges before we come to them? Do we not pour out the strength we shall need when the conflict comes, long before it arrives in anxious anticipation? So did Jesus. This is what Gethsemane shows us. Jesus is like us. And do we not crave someone with whom to share our troubles when they weigh more than we feel we can bear? So did Jesus. Is not this the explanation why he took three disciples into that garden? He needed human companionship, someone with whom he could talk, someone who might be presumed to understand. Loneliness is loneliness indeed when you are in trouble. But his disciples failed him. While he agonized they fell asleep. Do not blame them. Pity them. They were not callous, they were exhausted. All the same, the poignancy of Jesus coming over to their recumbent, perhaps snoring, forms seeking fellowship and finding none must stand. What is more, the situation was an indication of how it would be throughout the entire conflict about to begin. It would not be a case of the enemies of Jesus versus Jesus and his followers, but of the enemies of Jesus versus Jesus alone, his followers out of the struggle.

That he found this loneliness all but unbearable brings him close to every one of us. We know a little how he felt. He knows how much we feel.

3. What was the agony?

What was the agony? Need you ask? Is it not obvious? Who could there be who would not crumple up at the prospect of torture as terrible as crucifixion? As I have said in another sermon, I have often wondered if Jesus had seen a crucifixion. He would certainly know what it was like. The Romans saw to it that everyone knew. Crucifixion was that old world's deterrent against revolt by the people. You thought twice before you risked political action that might involve your being nailed up to a cross.

I do not suggest for one moment that the horror of what hung over Jesus was not one major reason for his agony. I have already made the point that he was a mortal man like us. But I do not think this is all. Jesus could have escaped. All the disciples made their getaway in the garden. And if the suggestion is too much that he might have jumped the garden wall likewise, nevertheless, escape was possible up to the moment of the arrest party arriving. It needs to be remembered that there were hundreds of people up for the festival for whom Jesus was a hero. Had they not lined the route to Jerusalem on Palm Sunday demonstrating their acclaim? There were supporters in plenty ready to hide him, and there were places in plenty in which to hide. Most of us have read in recent years of escape stories from situations far more shut in than these. What about Colditz? Yet Jesus did not escape. It is in that fact I suggest that a large part of the agony lies. He *could* have escaped. He *wanted* to escape. Who wouldn't, knowing what was coming? He entreated his heavenly Father in prayer that it might be right for him to escape; but since there was no sign from heaven, he knew for certain that the ministry entrusted to him would fail utterly if he did escape when his opponents closed in for the kill. The ministry that was peculiarly his involved a kill. There might be a way out, had he not been entrusted with a ministry. There was no way out, if he were to fulfil that ministry. The agonizing choice was his. He took it. He walked straight and deliberately into the hands of his enemies. He accepted the kiss of the traitor Judas, cursing neither him nor Peter who, in a matter of hours, swore that he had never known him.

But is there no more to the agony? I think there is but I do not know how to capture it in words. Something more was going on in that garden beyond the mortal struggle of a man facing a cruel death alone. Cosmic, not to say demonic, powers were fighting for this man's soul; for this man, if the interpretation of his life and work which the New Testament provides is anywhere near the truth, was to die a death for the sin of the world and to bear it away. Is it conceivable that such a cosmic deliverance could be accomplished without a conflict of cosmic agencies, good and bad, concentrated at one place and point in history – the garden of Gethsemane? And have we not here the reason why the unruffled dignity and calm which many have shown in face of death, not least many a Christian martyr including Blandina, the slave girl (AD 177 at Lyon), was for a while absent in the case of Jesus? I think so. I am however out of my depth here. Who isn't out of his depth here? All I can do is to stand by in utter reverence as one who believes in him. Here is my Saviour struggling and waging war against the evil in the world for the sake of the world, and for me. I cannot explain. I can scarcely describe, I can at best accept and bid you in your wisdom to do the same.

22. On Trial

Luke 22.66–69 (RSV)   *When the day came, the assembly of the elders of the people gathered together, both chief priests and scribes; and they led him away to their council, and they said, 'If you are the Christ, tell us'. But he said to them, 'If I tell you, you will not believe; and if I ask you, you will not answer. But from now on, the Son of Man shall be seated at the right hand of the power of God.'*

On the second page of his fascinating study called *Christian England* (Vol 2) David Edwards, the author, has this striking sentence 'Never in English history did preachers occupy more influential pulpits'. And when you look to see what they were there is nothing about cathedrals or royal chapels, or even vast attentive congregations, but rather stakes stuck in the ground piled round with faggots. They were places of execution by burning alive. And because the wood was often green, the rushes soggy, and dry gunpowder lacking (which might have provided a touch of mercy) there was nothing to prevent the utterance of last words as well as agonizing screeches of pain. What those dying men said under those conditions could not fail to be heard and be remembered and influence. This was the mid-sixteenth century; and the martyrs were not only Protestants like Latimer and Ridley testifying to their faith but Roman Catholics also such as Edmund Campion, the Jesuit, condemned to death in 1581.

1. Jesus's trial

Jesus had such a pulpit. It was on the eve of Good Friday when 'the assembly of the elders of the people gathered together, both chief priests and scribes; and they led him away to their council' determined to execute him. There they made this request: 'If you are the Christ tell us.' It was really a loaded question. Jesus's accusers knew it and he knew it. All along throughout his ministry in Galilee and Judaea, although time and time again he had spoken and acted in a messianic manner, he had never openly given himself out as the Messiah. But now with the executioner's axe, as it were, poised over his head, he answered their question clearly and boldly – 'From now on, the Son of Man shall be seated at the right hand of the power of God'. No pulpit Jesus could occupy could be more influential than that dock in the court room that day where he was condemned to death, or that cross where the actual execution took place. What he said was remembered, and for influence there has been nothing like it.

Let us listen for a moment to what he did say in the condemned dock. It is surprising, at first hearing even puzzling. 'From now on, the Son of Man shall be seated at the right hand of the power of God.' But *it is what happened*. The power of God did flow, does flow, from the crucified Jesus as never before or since, whatever mighty works were done by him in Galilee or Judaea and in his name throughout the world. The cross of Christ is powerful as nothing else is powerful.

Sometimes we can catch little glimpses of this sort of power in this century. During the last war a Canadian doctor called Ben Wheeler found himself a prisoner-of-war after the fall of Singapore in 1942. The conditions were appalling. Twenty hospital patients crammed into a room for six was typical, so close together that he had to crawl to reach them. Working under conditions like this he lost three stone in weight in the first year, and contracted beriberi and diarrhoea so badly that six visits a day and two at night to filthy latrines scarcely sufficed to relieve his misery. Yet barely a day passed without him visiting his sick patients in the camp. There were no medicines, none at all; and such operations as could be carried out were done with 'Do-it-yourself' instruments. For hours this doctor would talk seeking to revive hope in wretches who longed for nothing so much as to die. It is surprising that the general run of soldiers referred to him as 'the man sent from God', and a book has just been published with just that title? Power flows from a man who fulfils his ministry when death stares him in the face. That is how it was with Jesus, only more, much more – the man sent from God.

2. Jesus proclaimed

Sometimes I guess, perhaps very often, people wonder why we Christians devote so much attention to the sufferings of Jesus. The question must arise when the prominence given to crosses and crucifixes in our churches is taken in. Is it really necessary in our troubled world with all that is going on in the Lebanon, the Iran/Iraq frontier, El Salvador, not to mention Afghanistan, to spend time reliving the offensive scenes in the court room in

Jerusalem when Jesus was in the dock – the mockery of the chained prisoner, the clouting and the spitting. Must we really traipse along the *via dolorosa* to that dump of wasteland outside the city to see a man tormented, tortured and twisted till he is unrecognizable, a contortion of flesh and protruding bones foul with blood and excrement? But the point of looking and listening here is to see the real Jesus, because we shall only see him and hear him as he really is under such conditions. This is why we have the crucifixion narrative in all four gospels. They are there not to supply a point by point account of the trial or to present a macabre picture of what a crucifixion was like, but to proclaim Jesus as from a pulpit so that we know what manner of man he was.

And what manner of man was he? Well, look for a moment at the court scene. Peter, his chief disciple, was there but secretly. He had slunk into the yard below the court room to see the end. Standing by a burning brazier, incognito so he supposed, a serving girl accused him too loudly for his safety. So flatly he denied all knowledge of Jesus. Again and yet again he was charged by others, and not feeling sufficiently secure with these disavowals, he piled on the swearing and the curses he had apparently not forgotten how to use. From above in the court room Jesus saw and heard. He could have called out, 'You traitor, you liar'. But to do so would have implicated Peter, sending him to the gallows as well. So he simply looked. It was enough. You can tell what manner of person a man is, when he is concerned to save even a traitor from a cruel fate like his own.

And another incident, this one from the crucifixion itself. With a delicate reticence the evangelists refrain from describing the horrors of the nailing of Jesus to the cross and the final hauling of it into the terrifying upright position. One wonders what mien the faces of the men who did it portrayed. I read somewhere once, of a woman imprisoned by the Nazis in Vienna, that what plagued her more than the privations and punishments she suffered was the leering brutality of the faces that stood over her inflicting them. Was it like this with Jesus? If so, what would be more indicative of the manner of man he was than that he should utter then, 'Father forgive them for they know not what they do'.

So I say we look at Jesus the prisoner today and at his being crucified, so that we can see for ourselves and hear what manner of man he was, an aim entirely different from unhealthy morbidity. And what we see is someone who in the court room testified as from a pulpit that he was the Christ of God seated at the right hand of the power of God, caring not for himself but for others, even for a liar denying all acquaintance with him, even for men with cruel faces nailing him to his cross of torture. What does this tell us about the Messiah? What does it tell us about Christ? What does it tell us about the heart of God? Surely a message to comfort every one of us.

3. The Church on trial

Perhaps there is one other way in which we ought to look at the trial scene of Jesus when 'the assembly of the elders of the people gathered together, both chief priests and scribes; and they led him away to their council'. In a sense Christ is on trial today in the person of his Church. And not only here in his official representative body before the world but also in every individual who professes to be a Christian. How do we show up to our contemporaries? What manner of disciples of Christ do we appear to be?

I have been reading recently of the steadfastness and the courage of Christians in Russia. In spite of the penalties for taking this stand there is a growth of Christian discipleship in the Soviet Union chiefly at the two extremes of society, the intellectuals at one end and the simple country folk at the other. As I read I could not help wondering how faithful we are here in the West. Do we really reflect the Christ we profess or do we betray him?

At once perhaps our minds run to compassion. Christ was compassionate. Compassion was the outstanding mark of his ministry even to his final breath. Compassion is an 'in' word now. Political parties with no particular altruistic reference make judgements on policies from the angle of compassion or lack of it. This is not to say compassion needs no emphasis now. It desperately needs to be put into practice with policies for our depressed areas, not least the inner cities. There is however a harder test to be applied. Is the Church on trial today for faithfulness to the standards for which Christ stood? Does it take its stand by them? But who wants to hear what he said about divorce? Who is ready to advocate obedience as the road to happiness? Who talks of discipline as essential? Who, in a day when broadmindedness is so popular and all is to be forgiven, has ears for Christ's words from the sermon on the mount 'the gate that leads to life is small and the road is narrow'. Who dares *not* to hedge about pre-marital sex? Which pulpits proclaim sacrifice? Who is willing for Christ's sake to be different?

When we come again to Good Friday we have to ask this question. Is it possible to follow Christ and avoid the cross? It is a hard question and maybe we do not altogether like it when it is brought home. But it looks as if the Church gains more adherents when it stands firm and suffers than when it compromises and is smiled upon. The truth is there is iron in the gospel of Christ as well as compassion and Good Friday bids us hear this preaching from the pulpit of his cross. Dare we listen?

23. Darkness and Light

Mark 15.33 (RSV) *And when the sixth hour had come, there was darkness over the whole land until the ninth hour.*

I wonder if you have ever been in a situation where the outlook for the future was so dark you called it 'black'. I remember some years ago driving down Harley Street in London and pulling up at a cross-roads to let a couple pass in front of my car. They walked close to the bonnet. They were middle-aged, well-dressed, even fashionable. The woman was struggling desperately and unsuccessfully to stifle her sobs; and the man, presumably her husband, looked as if a good cry might ease his tension if only he could. My wife sitting beside me remarked 'I wonder what they have just heard. After all, this is Harley Street'. Had some medical consultant round the corner just provided them with a hopeless diagnosis? If so there was darkness over their whole land from that hour. Their whole life was out of joint.

1. The darkness of man's inhumanity to man

I cannot tell you if the darkness which crept over the whole land (the Greek could read 'whole earth') from the sixth to the ninth hour on Good Friday, that is from twelve noon till three o'clock, when Jesus was crucified – I cannot tell you if it was due to some natural phenomenon. It might perhaps have been caused by the Sirocco, the hot wind from Africa which can blow up in springtime so dust laden that it makes day seem like night. It could perhaps have been a freak rain storm. An eclipse is not a possible explanation because it was the time of the full moon and eclipses cannot occur then.

This, however, I do know that to see that man of all men, Jesus of Nazareth, pinned up to that cross that day was for anyone who knew anything about him at all a frightening foreboding that darkness was creeping over the whole human race; for Church and State, priests and people, civilians and the military had combined to do this thing. To what depths had mankind sunk? What tattered shreds of natural justice were left in the world? What in heaven's name had happened to religion that it could foul its hands with a contrived deed so dirty as the public and slow liquidation of Jesus?

And this is the terror of this darkness. It has not yet lifted from the world. Was there not a heading in at least one newspaper only a few weeks ago – 'Darkness gathers over the disarmament talks'? And if, as we sit here in this cathedral (York Minster) this afternoon, we could catch but a glimpse of what some relatively innocent men and women are suffering in Soviet labour camps now, and in prisons in Iran, Iraq, parts of Africa and South America – prisoners of conscience, religious minorities, political detainees, men and women whose only crime is that they wished to be free to express what they believed and what they thought – and if we knew to what extent sophisticated torture is employed to prise out wanted evidence; and if we dwell even for a moment on the millions deported to a certain death in this century, not to mention the wars, we would feel that darkness indeed had settled on the whole earth, the darkness of man's inhumanity to man which seems to know no bounds and never seems entirely to lift.

2. Darkness in the soul

There is another kind of darkness. I will call it darkness in the soul. So often it comes to individuals in face of some calamity.

I was in contact with a woman a few weeks ago whose long life has been one of consistent and cheerful Christian service to all kinds of people. She was, however, down in spirit as I have never known her to be. The external reasons were not difficult to trace. Unwell herself, she went with her husband for a short recuperative holiday in the United States, and to visit relatives, but there he suddenly died. Then she lost the sight of one eye as a result of a haemorrhage, to be followed by partial and growing blindness in the other. A keen water-colour artist and dressmaker, ever actively creative with her hands, all this would have to go. The small car, her great joy, had to be sold. The probability of transfer to a home weighed heavily – all this in twelve months. Is it surprising that God seemed far away? that faith in his providence faltered? Life scarcely seemed worth the candle. Yes, this is possible even for a sturdy Christian. How likely for many of us all before our earthly course is run.

The catalogue of calamities that may cancel out the light of life is heavy and long. Redundancy. Unemployment. Let-down by a marriage partner. The incidence of cancer. Business collapse. A sudden stroke. No job prospect. Examination failure. Loneliness. The loss of a limb. Housebound. Bedbound. . . I could go on. So could you. These are but some of the calamities that cloud over the soul, making all life dark. Is it possible to be buoyant then? Is it remotely possible? Yes, it is; and I have seen it. A kind of buoyancy is even returning to that woman of whom I spoke just now. Here, however, on this Good Friday there is this to remember. Jesus was *not* buoyant on the cross. He cried out in the darkness of what he felt to be divine abandonment 'My God, my God, why hast thou forsaken me?'

Here maybe, just here, is the first tiny pinpoint of light in the seemingly all embracing darkness of the crucifixion. Jesus, the external Son of God knew from experience what is meant by the darkness of the soul – if you like 'the dark night of the soul'. He knows it now. Everyone therefore who suffers can know that he, she, is not alone in the gloom. God indeed does not explain all. He does not relieve all. He did however, he does however, share all. You can't get much lower than the city dump where Christ was crucified, but God was there. O, the thousands upon thousands who have felt fellowship with the crucified in the prisons of life, physical, mental and spiritual down the centuries and been sustained thereby. It is not for nothing that a crucifix is hung on many a wall. It is not for nothing that some have scratched crosses on the walls of their cells, now a sobering sight for tourists when they encounter them.

So I speak directly now to anyone in darkness of soul. Do not despair. You are not alone. You are not really a God-forsaken person, whatever you feel. This is one message from Good Friday.

3. Theological darkness and light

There is however something bigger than this, something deeper, something broader. If we are to feel the power of the cross of

Christ we must not shrink from an attempt to think theologically.

From this angle, let it be said at once, the crucifixion of Jesus was at first almost total darkness. For the Jews who engineered it, that is to say the hierarchy of the day, his dying there in the same way as the blaspheming bandits on either side of him with no angel of God descending from heaven to rescue him, let alone prevent him from arriving there, was the final confirmation that he was *not* the Messiah. No wonder they ridiculed him as he died, jeered at him and spat out their bitter contempt. 'He trusted in God that he would deliver him, let him deliver him if he will have him.'

And there were people like Mary Magdalene and Mary the Mother of Joseph who stood afar off and watched, their hearts breaking. There were others like Cleopas who cried to themselves in their anguish 'We hoped that it was he which should redeem Israel'; but with his corpse on the cross before them all that hope was gone. There was nothing left but darkness.

To friend and foe alike the cross proclaimed nothing but proof that Jesus was not the Messiah. We however stand at another point in time. We look back at Good Friday from this side of Easter. We believe that the cross was not the end; the resurrection transformed it. Not that we need trouble with the crucifixion any more because there was a happy ending to a gruesome story, but because it completely alters the view of Messiahship Jesus's foes held and Jesus's friends held and the view we might ourselves hold of God too, *apart from the cross of Christ*. The Church came into being and exists today because the resurrection proved that the man on the cross was after all none other than the Messiah, the Christ of God, and those women and others standing afar off at the crucifixion scene were not deceived in feeling in their bones that he was indeed Messiah come to redeem the world.

And now the darkness begins to lift, the theological darkness. On that cross Jesus was accomplishing far more than suffering as man the torments inflicted by man, terrible as they were. He was bearing in his own soul the appalling weight of the sin of the world. No wonder it seemed as if even the divine presence was absent from that hateful scene, for sin always blots out the face of God, such is its nature. But God was there. God accomplishing his great redeeming work in Christ as St Paul put it so very neatly, 'God was in Christ reconciling the world to himself '.

So now we have a gospel of divine forgiveness. No, not simply that forgiveness is a nice idea so let us all forgive. That is feeble, and could be amoral if not immoral. No, the Christian gospel of forgiveness is based on Christ's work of bearing away the sin of the world. We may be free because of what he *has done* for us. He has dealt with our sin as our representative.

So the darkness lifts – 'there was darkness over the whole land *until the ninth hour*', not permanent darkness; in fact, in due course glorious light – and how different everything appears when the sun shines. Shapes which once terrified terrify no more. Pitfalls which might ensnare ensnare no more. Burdens we thought in the dark we should have to carry all our days we know now we need carry them not one single day longer.

Am I addressing anyone for whom the past casts its shadow right into the present, some foolishness, some misdoing, some degrading attitude leading to action of which we are now ashamed? My friend, turn the other way, the light is shining, shining from out of the darkness of the cross of Christ, He has borne all that past away, if only we will believe him.

24. It is Finished

'When Jesus had received the vinegar, he said "It is finished"' – that is what St John wrote (19.30 RSV). This is what St Luke wrote, *'Then Jesus, crying with a loud voice, said, "Father, into thy hands I commit my spirit."* And having said this he breathed his last.' (23.46 RSV).

So now we know. As the gospel writers have set out the narrative Jesus, as the end approached, said 'I thirst' in the hope that he might be given a sip of sour wine from the jar at the foot of the cross to enable him to cry out with a loud voice – *Tetelestai*, 'It is finished'. Thus Jesus ended his life as crucified men did not normally end their lives – on a cry of victory. But he knew that he had done it. He had accomplished the work his heavenly Father had given him to do. He had not deviated from a life of total obedience to the love of God and the love of men, never compromising, never breaking, never running away, faithful to the end though it cost him his life – God's servant, God's faithful servant, God's suffering servant – *Tetelestai* 'It is accomplished'.

The Roman centurion on guard standing opposite the cross knew nothing of mysteries such as these. But he knew how victims on crosses usually died. And this one on this Friday died differently from them all. Crucified victims hung as often as not, screaming till the voice gave out, and then they lingered a filthy, festering clot of flies sometimes for days, a living man whose hands and feet were swollen lumps of gangrenous meat. The centurion in charge was prepared for this. But it did not happen. Jesus, the man on the middle cross, retained his voice till the end; and the end came sooner than expected. And not only in his reckoning but in Pilate's too, when he was told. Jesus breathed his last about three o'clock with his going-to-bed prayer on his lips, the prayer from Psalm 31, the prayer of Compline 'Father, into thy hands I commend my spirit'. It looked, it sounded like a voluntary leave-taking when a task was finished. The centurion was startled, so startled that in his unthought-out comment he bore witness to the strangeness of this event, 'Truly, this was a son of God'.

1. What is finished

(a) His human life on earth

'It is finished.' What is finished? One answer of course, the most obvious, is that his life on earth was finished. But we need to pause here for a moment. We could never speak of Christ sharing our life if he did not share our death. To be a human being is to experience mortality. And death for a human being belongs to a different plane than is the case with plants and animals. Dead plants provide the compost for next year's growth. And there is a naturalness about the end of an animal's life that does not belong to human beings. For us death is an offence. It is a mockery of our powers, which are considerable. Yet the scientist able to plan a flight to the moon dies like any other creature. It is on account of the human spirit that death haunts the human being. And there is no way out in this life. No one can stop his own death. And Jesus could not stop his either. Not if he were to be a real man. So he died on the cross. 'It is finished.' His death made plain for all to see that he was a real human being, he was a man like us. We must never forget it or be tricked into explaining it away.

(b) His removal of any barriers between God and man

What is finished? There is no doubt that the writer of the fourth gospel, by including this saying in the account of Jesus's death, meant us to interpret it at a deeper level. So did St Mark, which is why he wrote 'And Jesus uttered a loud cry and breathed his last. And the curtain of the temple was torn in two from top to bottom.' No one is to be shut out of the presence of God now. The entrance stands wide open. Sin cannot shut anyone out. Colour cannot shut anyone out, nor class, nor income bracket, nothing that anyone has ever said or done or written in the past or present that was wrong is a *final* barrier. In surrendering his life in perfect obedience on the cross as our representative, sharing the whole of our life, including death, Jesus Christ has constructed the bridge of access to God, and peace of heart and mind for evermore. Nothing remains but for us to step on the bridge and cross it.

> Thou art the Way: by thee alone
> From sin and death we flee;
> And he who would the Father seek
> Must seek him, Lord, by thee.
>
> (Bishop G. W. Doane)

(c) The most severe attack of evil

'It is finished'. What is finished? The worst that the forces of evil can do is finished. There is nothing worse to be attempted than the liquidation of the Son of God; and it failed. We can see that it has failed, because here we are a Christian congregation gathered in this cathedral two thousand years later, paralleled by other worshipping Christian congregations throughout the world. Christianity is alive because Christ is alive, alive not merely in the sense remembered by law-worshippers but alive as a spiritual force, alive as God is alive. So evil, risking the worst it could do at Calvary, has been defeated. That battle is over. It is finished. Goodness has triumphed and will triumph.

Yet in a sense the battle is *not* over. It goes on still. It goes on in every man's and woman's life. It goes on in the world of our time, a desperate struggle, the struggle between good and evil, evil systems warring with eternal values. And the Church is in that struggle, struggling for the souls of people, struggling for the soul of what was once known as Christendom, struggling for its own soul. But the victory has been won. The issue is certain; good will triumph in the end. Evil has dealt its deadliest blow and been defeated. What remains is a long drawn out 'mopping up' oper-ation, a process continuing till the final day. From the vantage point of Christ's cross can be seen that final triumph there begun.

2. Jesus's last words

That complete triumph has not yet come. Just now we must return in imagination to the crucifixion in its closing moments and see Jesus's life moving swiftly to its close. Like most clergymen, I have been with the dying not infrequently. The experience subdues. Voices cannot be raised. And here on the cross, 'the Sun of righteousness with healing in his wings' is dying. What can we do but stay quite still. But he speaks. He recites the Psalms, which have been the mainstay of his life. Happy is the man or woman who has forms of prayer by heart in the final hour. We hear Jesus begin and end his prayer with 'Father'. 'Father, forgive them for they know not what they do.' 'Father, into thy hands I commend my spirit.' Or to go back to his very first recorded words as St Luke records them, 'Did you not know that I must be in my Father's house?' Jesus finished his life as he began it, in the consciousness of God as his Father, present at all times, present everywhere even at this ghastly execution plot. There is nothing greater any one of us can do, nothing more sustaining than to believe in God as Our Father. 'Our Father in heaven.'

Still we watch. There is no voice now. Presently his head fell. So far as life on this earth is reckoned it is finished.

There is a Chinese saying that a mother does not fear death after her little baby has died. I do not know the truth of this – how could I? – but certainly death is not the same since Jesus has died. Nothing is the same; not even the cemetery or the crematorium.

> 'O death, where is thy sting?
> O grave, where is thy victory?'

> 'Peace, perfect peace, death shadowing us and ours?
> Jesus has vanquished death and all its powers.'
>
> (Bishop E. H. Bickersteth)

The last words of Jesus remain in our ears, 'Father, into thy hands I commend my spirit'. It is with our hands that we hold things. They signify keeping power. So the hands of God mean his power to keep us. And Jesus said of those who are his, 'No one is able to pluck them out of my Father's hands'. What more right action then for us to take than to commit ourselves for life and death into our heavenly Father's hands. There we are safe.

Perhaps we might go further and use theological language, even pietistic language and affirm that we are saved. I believe we are. I believe that he who was impaled on the cross on Good Friday is the saviour of the world. At that place and in that event God was in Christ *saving*. I go further, I believe that what we see at Calvary is the outcrop of the tireless activity of God. There always has been and there always will be suffering activity at the heart of God 'for us men and our salvation'. The cross of Christ is a window on what God is like, a window on what God is for ever doing. Timothy Rees (1874–1939) put it well in the hymn when he wrote

> 'And when human hearts are breaking
> under sorrow's iron rod,
> Then they find that self-same aching
> deep within the heart of God.'

3. The appeal of Good Friday

So the appeal to us all this Good Friday, with the cross of Christ in imagination (stimulated by the gospel records) before us, is not merely to watch but to respond to the God who was there and reigns on high, 'Father, into thy hands I commend my spirit'. Then Christ will 'see of the travail of his soul and be satisfied'. And we shall be part of that great throng which began to form up at the foot of the cross even before Good Friday was over – 'a great multitude which no man could number from every nation, from all tribes and peoples and tongues . . . singing Amen! Blessing and glory and wisdom and thanksgiving and honour and power and might be to our God for ever and ever. Amen.'

25. The Grave

Mark 15.46 (NEB) *Then he laid him in a tomb cut out of the rock, and rolled a stone against the entrance.*

My sermon today is still about Jesus but not about anything he said or did but about that mortal body of his which was like ours. It came to be placed in a tomb cut out of the rock with a stone rolled against the entrance; exactly where we do not know. It remains the unknown grave.

I hope you will not count me morbid when I speak about this, but if I did not I should be unfaithful to the gospel accounts of Jesus because they all mention it more than in passing. The burial is important. It was important to those who had lived closest to him and who believed in him. And not simply because it has something to say to us about our funerals and graves but because the nature of Christian faith requires Jesus's burial as an article of belief. It is not for nothing that it stands in the creeds.

1. The burial of Jesus

In recent years we have seen funerals fairly frequently on the television, big funerals. Only last month St Luke's Church, Chelsea, a huge building, was filled from end to end, galleries and all, for the funeral of one young woman. She was the policewoman killed by the IRA bomb planted just before Christmas outside Harrods in London. But no week passes in Northern Ireland without funerals on this scale. All are for victims of violence. Jesus was a victim of violence. He had a grave but no funeral.

Yet he was buried. He was buried in a tomb as yet unused. It belonged to one called Joseph, originally from Arimathaea (wherever that may be). He took down the body of Jesus from the cross, though he could scarcely have done this alone. What he took down was nothing like those moving representations of the so-called 'Descent from the Cross,' such as Michaelangelo's in the Duomo in Florence. It was as unlike that of a child in his mother's arms as could be. It was a corpse similar to one left on a battlefield, from which the instinct is to turn away, ghastly, disfigured, knotted after pain, crumpled with gaping mouth and staring unclosed eyes. Joseph saw all this and hurried to a shop to purchase a sheet for a covering. Time was short, for the Sabbath was approaching. He wrapped the body round (the Greek consistently calls it 'him' not 'it'), laid him in a tomb cut out of the rock, conveniently close by the crucifixion site, and rolled the stone into place which blocked the entrance. There was no funeral but there was a burial. This is important. The crucified were frequently left on their crosses as a grim warning to the public. The method did not die with the Romans. London three to four hundred years ago, exhibited the heads of the executed on spikes on London Bridge.

But why did Joseph of Arimathaea provide for the burial of Jesus? He was not a follower but a well-to-do member of Jerusalem's supreme council. What made him risk a charge of being implicated with Jesus by begging for the body from Pilate? It took courage. He was no relative. The Romans did give permission to relatives to take down the bodies of the crucified. Was Joseph prompted merely by propriety? Jewish bodies ought not to remain exposed on the Jewish Sabbath, or was he a secret disciple as the fourth gospel says? We can understand if he was.

2. The burial is important

Come back to where I began. The burial is important. Why is it important? Because it shows a *caring attitude*. First of all for the human body. Take this man Joseph of Arimathaea. For him it was unthinkable that the body of Jesus should be ripped off the cross and tossed into the city incinerator, its most likely destination if no one came to claim it. But to Joseph that body was precious. Those hands had healed people. Those lips had spoken words of life to people. Through that body God had been brought close. How could it be cast aside of no account? That Joseph made provision that this should not happen shows that he understood how the body of every person, especially of this man, is – to use St Paul's words – a temple of the Holy Spirit. It must not be defiled.

I have heard of men and women – more often men – professing not to care about what happens to the body at death or the ashes after cremation. This non-caring attitude could indicate scepticism about eternal life. It could on the other hand indicate that what remains after death is not the person anyway. Nevertheless this body has been the place and medium in which, and by which, the spiritual (which is eternal) has not only existed but actually been made visible and tangible. Therefore it is wrong not to care for our bodies now. It is also wrong not to care what happens to them at death. That Joseph of Arimathaea provided a burial place for Jesus showed how highly he rated the human body and how much he cared.

Secondly the burial rites show that someone cares about us. So I draw your attention to those two women who from afar watched Joseph take down the body of Jesus from the cross, wrap it in a sheet, place it in his tomb and then roll the great stone against the entrance. One of them was Mary Magdalene. If I could paint I would paint a picture of those two women's faces. Perhaps some-one has. What anguish and what affection was mingled in those eyes! But why were they there? Because when they could do nothing they nevertheless showed that they cared. Funerals and burial rites at least fulfil this function, that they provide an opportunity to·show that someone cares. And when our time comes, as it surely will, and we are carried to the cemetery or crematorium, that people attend will show that we did not pass through this world wholly unappreciated. Someone cared.

Why was Jesus's burial important? I have left till the last the *theological reason* because most hangs on it for us. Jesus died the death we shall die and he was buried. The event as recorded in St Mark's gospel could not be more matter of fact, crying out its authenticity. *This is what happened.* Without the death which burial completes there would be no gospel of the risen Christ, and without that gospel no real gospel at all. But Joseph of Arimathaea 'laid him in a tomb cut out of the rock and rolled a stone against the entrance', two women watching. The end of Jesus as the man from Nazareth had come. That burial was the witness. But within three days there was another story to tell which is why we Christians now both weep and rejoice in the face of death, man's last enemy. We have a gospel to proclaim. Death is not the end. There is life to come.

26. Life in the Light of Easter

Mark 16.6 (NEB) *But he said to them, 'Fear nothing; you are looking for Jesus of Nazareth, who was crucified. He has risen; he is not here; look, there is the place where they laid him.'*

If you have imagination – and you must exercise imagination to appreciate the Easter story – you can see this tiny group of women to whom these words were addressed. You can see them gazing with frightened eyes in the half light of early dawn into that hole in the ground where the body of the one they loved had been buried. You can see them clutching precious little parcels of aromatic ointments with which to complete the burial rites for that more precious body they expected to find there. But there was nothing they could do. Nothing at all. All the hours in which they had busied themselves with practical activities as women do in a crisis, preparing those spices, were wasted. He wasn't there. The grave was empty, cold and hollow.

The poignancy of this emptiness has been sharpened by the writer of the fourth gospel by centring it on one of the women, Mary of Magdala. He writes, 'Early on the Sunday morning, while it was still dark,' she came to the tomb'. Putting the various accounts together – no easy task – it appears that it was only three o'clock, when presumably with the dawn the city gates would be opened, that this tiny group of women, among whom Mary of Magdala was prominent, 'knocked each other up' (as we say). Keeping together for safety's sake they stole along the silent streets out through the gate into the open ground beyond where they knew the garden tomb was situated. Mary, however, was emotionally incapable of restricting her pace to that of the older women. She ran. She couldn't help running. Her heart was near to breaking point. Tears were already starting down her cheeks. So she was the first in history to reach the place on Easter morning at which the whole history of mankind turns.

1. Jesus lights up the dark

I ask you to notice that the Easter story begins 'while it was still dark'. These women epitomize what our troubled life is like without Easter. It is dark. Not all the time. Let us be realistic. There are a thousand experiences we lightheartedly enjoy – food, holidays, the colour of the trees in spring, the meeting together of friends – the list is endless. But what when the bottom falls out of life? Then without Easter it is dark. It was for these women. Him whom they adored, who was all the world to them, now lay dead in a hole in the ground. Everything that gave meaning to life was over, over for ever.

Is this experience of pointlessness and meaninglessness unknown to us? Is it unknown in the twentieth century? What if nuclear warfare breaks out? What if redundancy becomes our lot? What about the young married woman who is told she cannot have children? What about the executive in the prime of life struck down with a stroke? What about bereavement? What about loneliness which goes on and on like a dull ache? Don't tell me you are not on the wavelength of Mary of Magdala and the other women, on Easter morning 'while it was still dark'. You are only half human if that is what you say. When life seems pointless because of what has happened, we do not live, we only exist, and when we only exist every day is dark; and when the days are dark as well as the nights, we grow terribly afraid. What will happen if...?

On Easter morning, however, these women out of whose eyes the light had gone heard these words at the most hurting place of their soreness, 'Fear nothing'. These are in fact the first words of Easter Day, 'Fear nothing'. And if they convey no more than an off-the-cuff call for courage in the face of heartbreak, they are offensive. Meaning cannot so cheaply be put back into meaninglessness. This can only be accomplished by an objective and external act which cuts off the root of meaninglessness. This is what the resurrection of the crucified Jesus did and does. 'Fear nothing; you are looking for Jesus of Nazareth, who was crucified. He has risen; he is not here; look, there is the place where they laid him.'

This is what Easter says first of all. Everything does not end in a hole in the ground or the crematorium gates. And because life is not *in the last resort* meaningless, it cannot be meaningless all the way along. That sacrifice you made which no one noticed, let alone appreciated, is not wasted. That setback you suffered, that letdown that nearly broke your heart, that incapacitating illness which struck you down – none of this is the useless rubbish of life. It means something. It points to something. It is not pointless. This is what Easter says to us 'while it is still dark'. 'Fear nothing.' Life is not 'a tale told by an idiot signifying nothing'. This we know when we come face to face with the truth of Easter as those women came face to face with it; and Peter and John too, and all the apostles, and the whole believing Church from that day till now, wherever its faith is exercised.

2. Jesus is essentially different

Secondly, we are not to fear 'while it is still dark' that Jesus of Nazareth for all his startling actions and impressive personality – that healing of the leper for instance, that sermon on the mount, that sitting down with 'publicans and sinners' maddening to Pharisees, that astonishing teaching in parables never surpassed, that transfiguration on the mountain top – we are not to fear that he was not essentially different from any other world religious leader but only relatively different, different in degree (one world religious leader is roughly similar to every other world religious leader; you can take your pick, it matters little). This is not so.

But why should we fear the charge that he was not essentially different? Because, if he was not, then in his particular case the worship of him by millions the world over is exceedingly hard to explain. And for this reason. By normal standards at the close of his life and work there was so little to show. Not surprisingly, for both life and ministry were so short in duration and carried out in a backwater. Moreover he acquired so few committed followers, and they deserted him at the end, at least the men deserted. He wrote no book, set up no organization, laid down no rules. The manner of his death was a disgrace and meant to be by those who engineered it. All that was left was a tiny group of frightened women clutching little parcels of aromatic spices come to the hole in the ground where he got buried, come to perform some last pathetic rites.

Why then the myriads of worshippers today? Why the Church in all the world transcending national and cultural barriers? Certainly not because after his death people came together and said 'Let us form an organization to commemorate this wonderful man. Let us hallow the place where he was buried.' We don't even know where it was! Even the women who did know on Easter morning found nothing there. 'He is not here. Look, there is the place where they laid him.' No, Jesus is worshipped because he rose from the dead. Not that anyone can prove it from the resurrection stories, nor for that matter can anyone disprove it. But the whole New Testament is alive with the confession 'He is risen'. Without that there would be no New Testament, and no Church either, and no Christian prayers, nor hymns, nor Christian ethic which even modern humanists respect. Easter begins in the dark with a supposed dead Jesus; but the light of the risen Christ so came to fill the sky that day that no darkness has ever been able to overtake it. Why? Because Jesus is essentially different. There is nothing to fear. He is worthy of our worship now and always for he is the Lord.

3. Jesus is the light of Easter

So we look now at Jesus 'while it is still dark' but in the broad daylight of Easter. This is how the gospel authors wrote of him. Not simply as a man only far better, though his humanness was genuine enough; but he was so *essentially different* when seen in the light of the resurrection that both Matthew and Luke tell of a virgin birth, Mark in his opening sentence labels him 'Son of God', and the fourth gospel depicts him as the Word of God through whom all that came to be was 'alive with his life and that life was the light of men'.

Therefore the Church tells the story of Jesus not only as the man from Nazareth who is worth our respect but as the one in whom and through whom God is made known. This is the proper way to preach through the life of Christ. He is not dead. A dead Christ is nowhere to be found. But the living Christ is everywhere to be found, not least in the hearts, yes, even in the faces, of those who believe in him.

Let me end with an up-to-date story from Soviet Russia. It comes from Michael Bourdeaux's arresting book *Risen Indeed* (pp. 41, 42). He describes how he was standing in a church in total darkness packed with people for the Easter service. Outside a procession encircled the building symbolically searching for the body of Christ. All at once there sounded a distant, mournful chant. Then a great hammering on the door at the back of the building. It creaked open. Next voices were raised in these responses:

> Whom seek ye?
> The body of Jesus
> Why seek ye the living among the dead?
> He is not here. He is risen – *Khristos voskrese*
>
> And the great crowd broke its silence
>
> *Voistinu voskrese* (Is risen indeed)

The rest must be told in Michael Bourdeaux's own words.

'But now too there was light. Someone at the back had lit the first paschal candle, a single point of light not able to penetrate the darkness. But then there was another, and another. Swiftly the flame passed from hand to hand. I began to see what I had not known. Every one of the worshippers held a candle. In less than a minute the church was a blaze of light – no, not the impersonal glare of electricity – it was five thousand individual flames united in one faith. Each candle lit up a face behind it. That face bore the deep lines of sorrow, of personal tragedy. Yet, as it was illuminated, the suffering turned to joy, to the certain knowledge of the reality of the risen Lord. Seeing my empty hands an old lady reached out to me across the low rail. I could hardly hear her say, "*Khristos voskrese*", above the exultant shouts that now came from the worshippers, but as I replied I felt the barriers of nationality and culture fall away. I was one of them.'

Appendix

The following Sundays, four days in Holy Week, the Transfiguration and a Church Dedication Festival have sermons in the foregoing pages based on the scripture readings appointed for Years 1 or 2 or for both years in The Alternative Service Book. Most of the readings constitute the Gospel for the Eucharist but four are based on Evensong second readings. On four occasions the sermon follows a parallel gospel passage marked thus II.

	Year	Sermon
Advent 2	2	7
4	2	1
Christmas 2	1	2
Epiphany 1	1 E	3
2	1	6
	2	5
6	1 & 2	11
Palm Sunday	1 & 2 II	15 & 23
Holy Week, Monday	1 & 2	20
Tuesday	1 & 2 II	21 & 22
Good Friday	1 & 2	24
Easter Eve	1 & 2 II	25
Easter	1 & 2	26
Easter 1	2	12
Pentecost 1	2 E	4
6	2	14
10	2	10
12	2	8
15	2 E	17 & 18 II
18	2 E	9
Last Sunday	2	19
Transfiguration		13 II
Dedication of a Church		16